QUILTS FROM A DIFFERENT ANGLE

by Sara Nephew

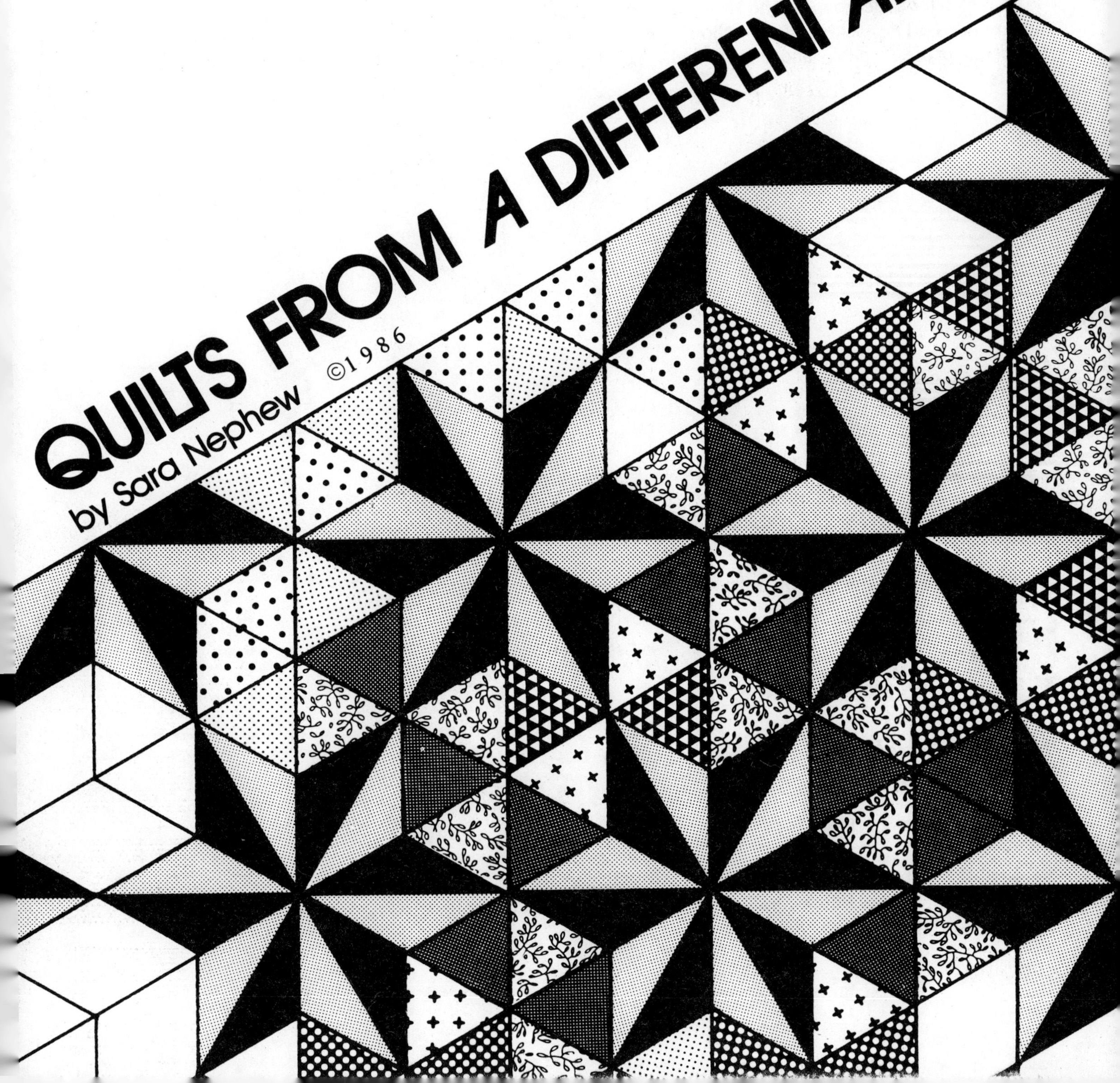

ACKNOWLEDGEMENTS

I dedicate this book to the people who encouraged me most: my husband, my parents, and two supportive friends, Diane Coombs and Rose Herrera. Each time I slowed down, somebody got me going again.

Thanks to the members of the Busy Bee Quilters and Quilters Anonymous. The company of fellow quilters and access to teachers, professionals, and artists help develop everyone's talents.

CREDITS

Photography . . . . Carl Murray
Illustration and Graphics . . . . Stephanie Benson

All quilts made by the author unless otherwise noted.

QUILTS FROM A DIFFERENT ANGLE©

ISBN: 0-943574-40-4

CONTENTS

INTRODUCTION

While making Log Cabin wall hangings to sell, I began experimenting with new designs and methods. I drafted a 60° diamond with strips going in two different directions. Then I realized that assembly would be easier if I separated the diamond into two different triangles.

Leaving the Log Cabin behind, I began to explore the design possibilities. I redrew some engineering graph paper that had what seemed like a million tiny triangles on it, making more sheets on a copy machine. When I sat down with my colored pencils, I was soon joined by my daughter, then my smallest son, and finally even my teenaged son for awhile. We were having fun!

I devised a guide for my rotary cutter out of two 60° triangles from the stationery store. People liked the designs and soon I was teaching a class. Encouraged by friends, I turned my class notes into this book. My hope is that people who try these methods have as much fun as I am having, and themselves discover some new designs.

All the quilts in this book are made from equilateral triangles. The equilateral triangle has a 60° angle in each corner and three equal sides. Combine this with what we call strip-piecing and sandwich-piecing, a rotary cutter, and new graph paper, and suddenly wonderful new designs start appearing. Moreover, some traditional designs can be pieced much more quickly or given a new look if you like.

There are designs in this book for the beginner and for the more advanced quilter. Anyone can learn the techniques, and if they want to, they can experiment with new designs on graph paper or with fabric. Most traditional quilt blocks are based on 90° and 45° angles, probably because paper folds easily into these divisions, and design and drawing tools were often primitive. How much more we now have to work with!

Quilts From A Different Angle is comprised of two sections. The first section explains the techniques and construction of equilateral triangle quilts. Begin by reading the entire book to get a general idea of the designs and techniques covered. Skim if you are anxious to get started, but do take the time to familiarize yourself with this exciting new process. You may want to make copies of the triangle graph paper to design some original work of your own. If you wish, you can go directly to fabric to learn the techniques.

The pattern section of the book begins on page 33. There are directions and diagrams provided for 11 different quilt designs in various sizes along with general directions for construction of the quilt.

My hope is that once you become familiar with these techniques you will confidently make your own changes in the patterns, adapting them to your needs by choosing a different size triangle, adding or subtracting blocks and rows, or adding borders. Some of the projects shown in the color photos illustrate the results of these changes.

I also hope you enjoy this book and produce some beautiful quilts of your own design from triangles.

QUILT DESIGN

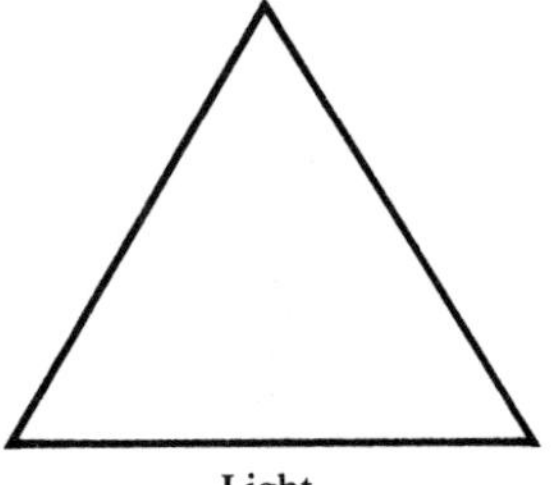
Light

EQUILATERAL TRIANGLES

The shape we are working with is the equilateral triangle. It can be colored and divided in a number of different ways.

1. Dark and Light Combinations
2. Line(s) Parallel with the Base (on base triangles)
3. Line(s) Perpendicular to the Base
4. Divided in Half Either Parallel or Perpendicular
5. Change of Scale

These shapes are then repeated and combined to form designs. Since these design ideas are new, you probably can't tell which ones you like. So draw them on paper first, maybe trying different colors and arrangements, until you get one you like.

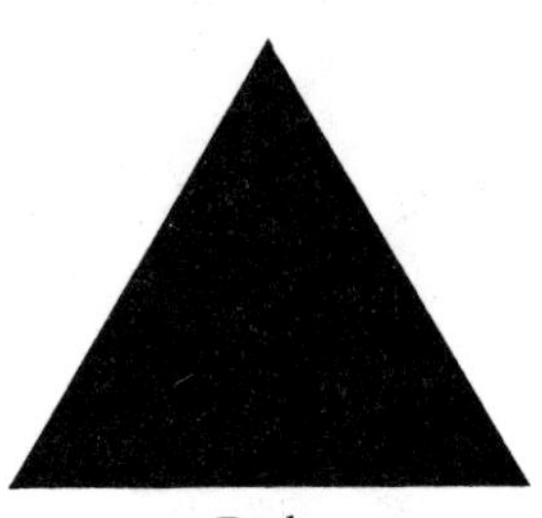
Dark

Parallel with base

Perpendicular to base

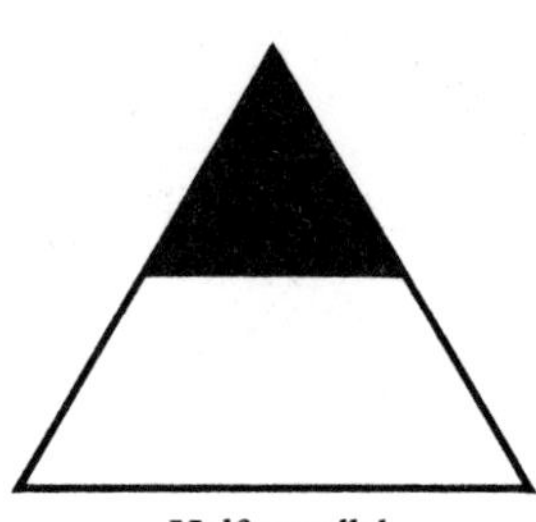
Half parallel

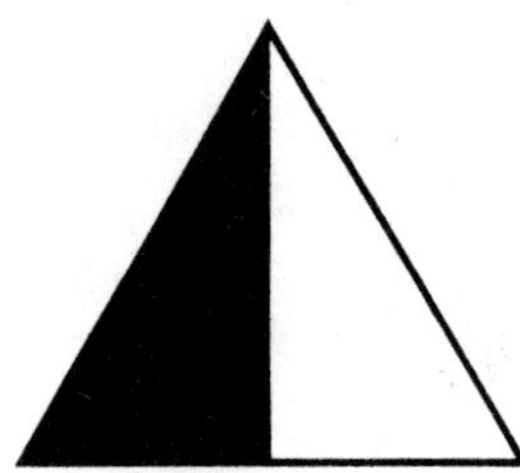
Half perpendicular

Change of scale

To begin designing, first choose the triangle you want to use. Then do a sketch on graph paper of one or all of these basic arrangements:

1. Six pointing out
2. Six pointing in
3. Six pointing out—three in each direction
4. Three pointing out and three pointing in
5. Six lined up in a row
6. Eight arranged in a diamond
7. Combine three of your original triangle design with three of another design and arrange as in numbers 1—6.
8. Try a four and two combination and arrange as in numbers 1—6.
9. Try a five and one combination of two different triangles and arrange as in numbers 1—6.

Keep your eyes open for an attractive pictorial or repeat design. Consider putting a printed or applique picture in the empty space of a plain triangle.

Then, start making larger arrangements with one of the above as your beginning. Add rows around the center to make a concentric design. Add triangles to shape your center into a diamond, star, triangle, or hexagon. On graph paper splash down parts and variations of your design in a pleasing arrangement, a little bit here and a little bit there. Try combining large and small versions of your design. When you have a substantial beginning to your design, stop and evaluate it. Is there a weakness that makes you dislike it? What could you do to correct and improve it? Try any or all of the design arrangements on the next page, using the triangle(s) you chose.

Triangle Choice

6 pointing out

6 pointing in

6 pointing out, 3 in each direction

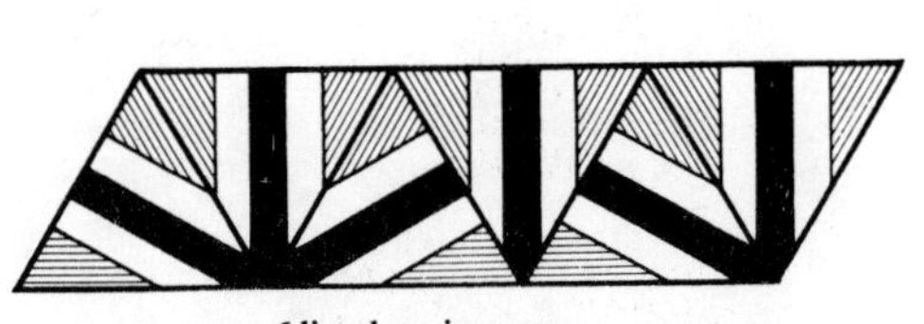

6 lined up in a row

8 arranged in a diamond

3 pointing in and 3 pointing out

There are many basic design approaches:

1. All Over

2. Repeat

3. Concentric

4. Striped

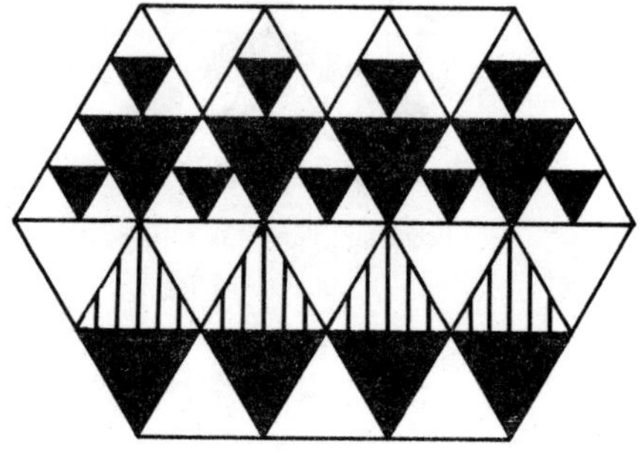

5. Assymetrical

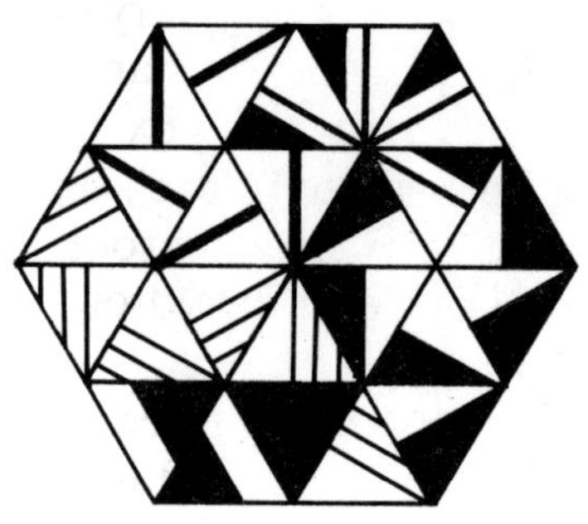

6. Pictorial

7. Change of Scale

Any one idea you have may work in any of these arrangements. The best way to evaluate a design is to sketch it out, using different values, colors, and sizes of graph paper.

COLOR

This is a color wheel in the shape of a hexagon star. The primary colors are red, yellow, and blue. Between the primaries are the colors you get when you mix them. Each of these is the complementary color to the primary color opposite it on the color wheel. On either side of the star points of the primaries are the colors you get when you mix the primary with the complementary color on that side.

Example: red + purple = maroon
red + orange = red-orange

Good color schemes are:
Primary—any or all of these three colors together
Complementary—a primary and its opposing triangle
Analagous—any triangle that includes a star point, 3 colors included, plus any half-hexagon that includes any 3 star points.

Any color or combination can be varied in shades and tints. You can extend any of these color schemes even farther by adding white or black, or both. So any color scheme has six additional variations.

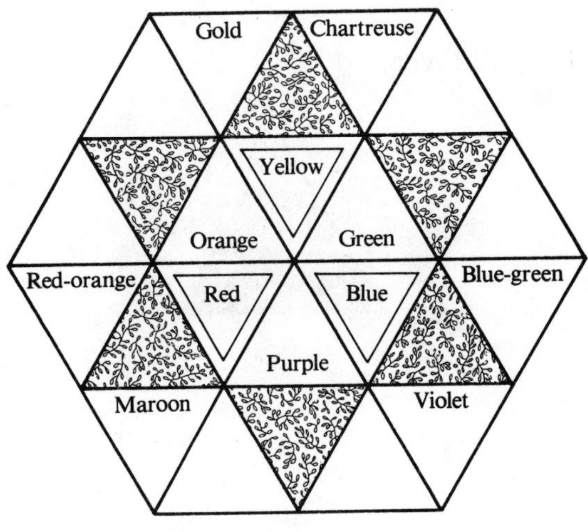

3 Color Analagous

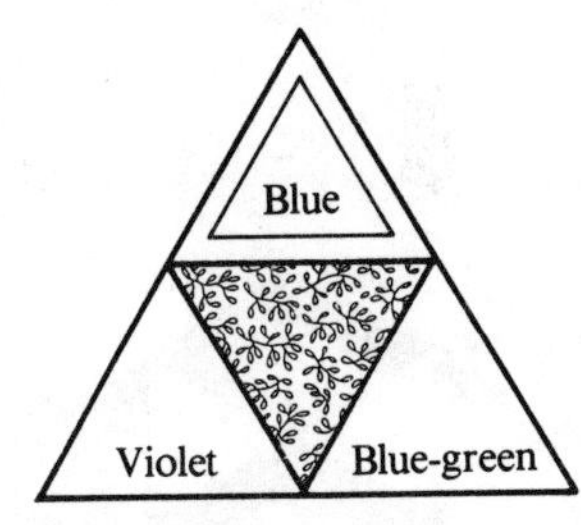

5 Color Analagous

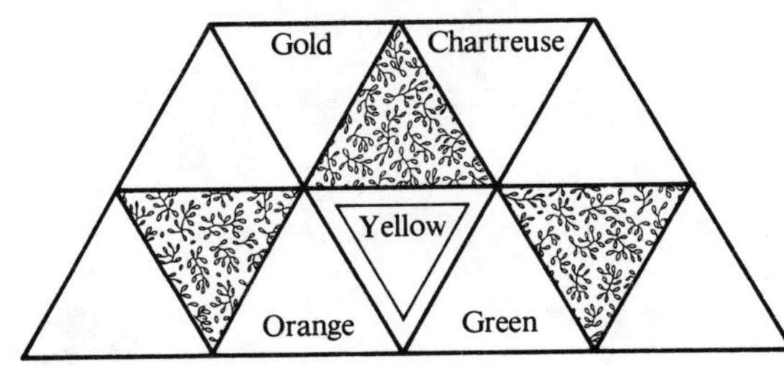

7 Color Analagous

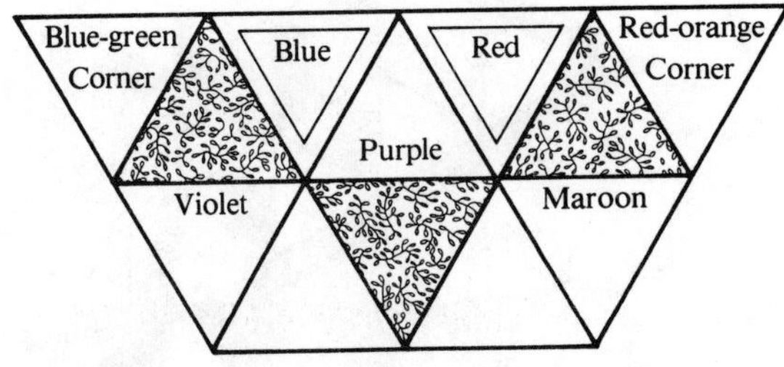

If you need to make this easier to handle, omit the 2 corner colors, or use only one, as an accent.

Examples:

Monochromatic Color Scheme

Color: Red

1. Red + White
2. Red + Black
3. Red + Black + White
4. Shades and tints of Red + Black + White
5. Shades and tints of Red + Black
6. Shades and tints of Red + White

Complementary Color Scheme

Colors: Red + Green

1. Red + Green + White
2. Red + Green + Black
3. Red + Green + Black + White
4. Shades and tints of Red + Green + Black + White
5. Shades and tints of Red + Green + Black
6. Shades and tints of Red + Green + White

The amounts and choice of color and the strength and weakness of the colors will cause some parts of your design to stand out and others to blend into the background. The colors chosen can greatly help the illusion of reality in a pictorial quilt.

Colors can be parallel to tastes in the mouth or feelings. A color or combination of colors can be: sweet, acid, sour, mellow, wild, quiet, contemplative, or sick. It is possible to have too much of a good thing. A color combination can be too sweet or too mellow (as when browns and golds are chosen to go with everything) or too exciting. (Can't sleep under that quilt? Can't even stay in the same house with it.) Color sophistication is a combination of education and experience. So don't be afraid to experiment...sometimes. Other times, use your favorite colors to make your quilt a pleasure to work with.

When planning a color scheme, you seldom want to use your colors all at equal strength and value. You might use one bright and pure, one shaded, and one a tint. And you might use an abundance of one color and just a little dab of another, rather than even amounts. This is where your judgment and feelings are involved. This is where you can use instinctive artistry.

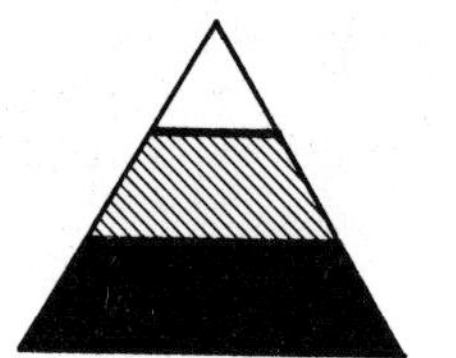

Color value can be a very important element of your design. Triangles divided into light, medium, and dark sections can be used to:

1. Make an effective showcase.

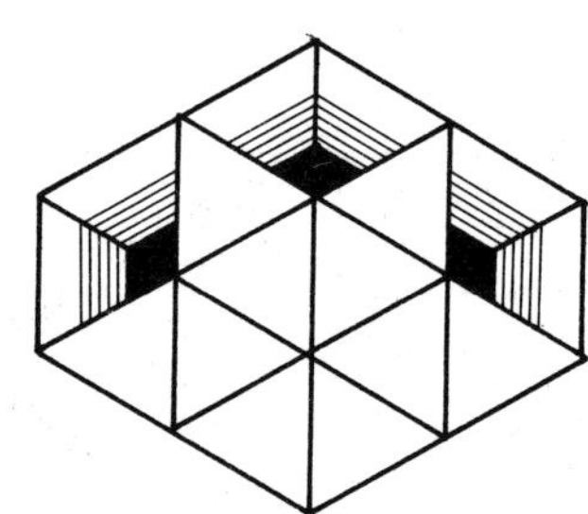

2. Make a directional flow with an effect of transparency.

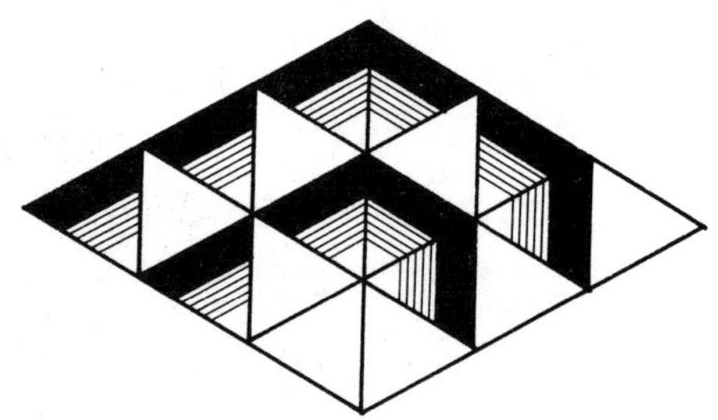

3. Add 3-dimensional effect.

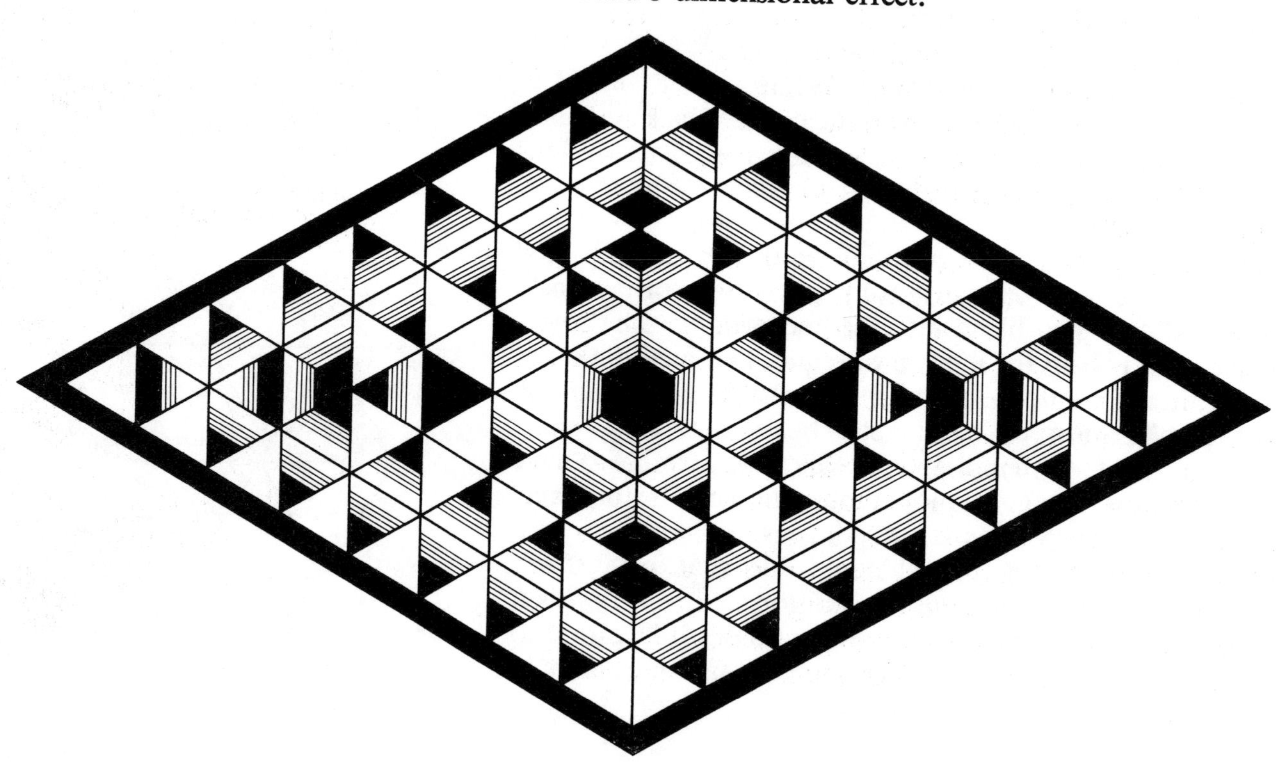

FABRIC

When learning these techniques, many quilters seem to prefer to go directly to fabric, rather than sketch designs. There is much to be learned this way, and we all love cloth. Here are a few fabric hints which you might find helpful.

My own collection is 100% cotton. If I need one particular color that is available only in a blend, I buy as much as I need for this one use. I prefer cotton because you can always iron at the same temperature with a dry iron, which is lighter. This avoids a sore arm and also tends to eliminate overpressing. When necessary, a wet press cloth and hot iron will flatten any part or all of a cotton quilt top perfectly. Also, cotton is the easiest to quilt and feels soft, light, and airy. It doesn't hold grease stains and doesn't pill. We are familiar with how cotton ages and know how to care for it.

All of my fabric is washed by hand in hot, soapy water to see if it is colorfast and dried in a hot dryer to shrink it. If the fabric color stains a test fabric after rinsing, cook it in soapy water in an enamel or stainless steel pot. Almost any soap will do, from laundry detergent to rug shampoo. Simmer a while, rinse and test again. When it no longer bleeds into the test fabric, it's safe to use in your quilt.

The most important rule when using prints, is to mix different sizes of patterns to prevent boredom. It is also interesting to mix prints and solids. I like to have the patterns add to the theme. All the different prints in the Snowstorm wall hanging look like snowflakes seen both up close and from a distance. Let the detail add to the overall effect.

Directional fabrics, such as stripes, plaids, and polka dots can be wonderful. Just be careful and thoughtful when using them. Lay out your pieces and look at them to see if what you are planning will work. Make choices rather than unknowingly letting it happen. I would rather use a design with some life in it, and some mistakes, than a technically perfect quilt that's all choked up in color and pattern. Have some fun! You only live once!

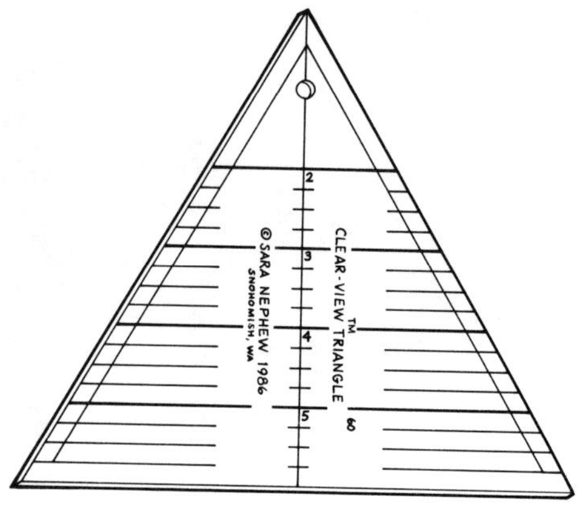

TEMPLATES

New techniques require new tools. The Clear-View Triangle was designed especially for the methods described in this book and is a great help in making 30°, 60°, and 120° angles. It is an acrylic triangle which has the proper thickness for use with a rotary cutter. The Clear-View Triangle has a dark perpendicular line and graduated 1", 1/2", and 1/4" rulings parallel with the base. As an additional feature, seam lines are indicated. This template is available in 6" and 12" size. See page 48 for ordering information.

You can also make a template yourself, using a minimal amount of tools. Start with two 6" 60° triangles, easily obtainable from the drafting section of a stationery or art supply store. Place the two perpendicular sides of the triangles together and tape firmly, using transparent packaging tape (2" wide). Tape both sides. Trim edges and holes with scissors. Then, using a see-through ruler and a permanent marking pen, mark lines 1" apart up from the base. To make these lines more permanent, scratch them in with a scribe or big needle. You can make larger templates with 8" and 10" triangles.

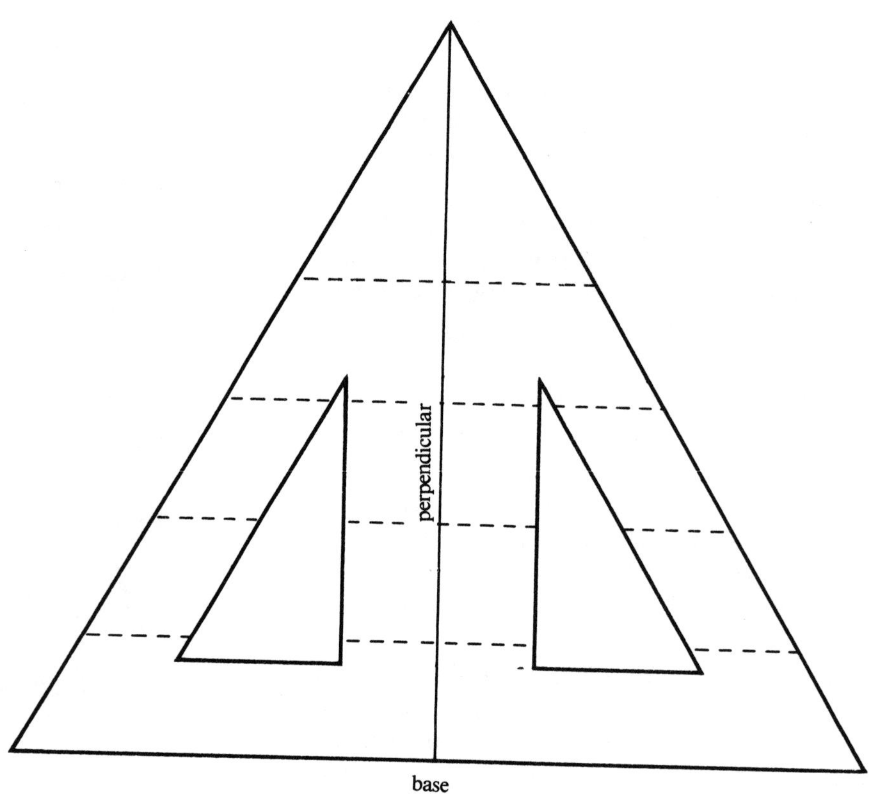

Other Sizes and Shapes

You can use your templates to get the correct angles on larger background pieces, triangles, diamonds, and parallelograms. On page 41 is the pattern for the wall hanging, Snowstorm. You can see the background pieces that were cut out of large pieces of cloth, rather than pieced from small triangles. Use your largest template for accuracy.

To cut shapes to fill in backgrounds, borders, or otherwise complete a design, you can see which angles will be needed in your design; it is not necessary to actually measure degrees.

Draw all the angles needed. Complete the shape of your fill-in piece. Check the measurements of the sides. Be sure to include seam allowances. If you are matching a section already constructed, measure this section. If it is an edge piece, I often cut it larger and trim it after I sew it on, checking angles with my template.

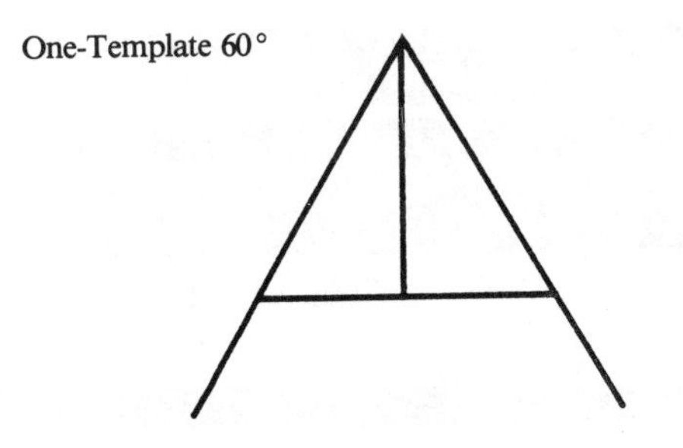

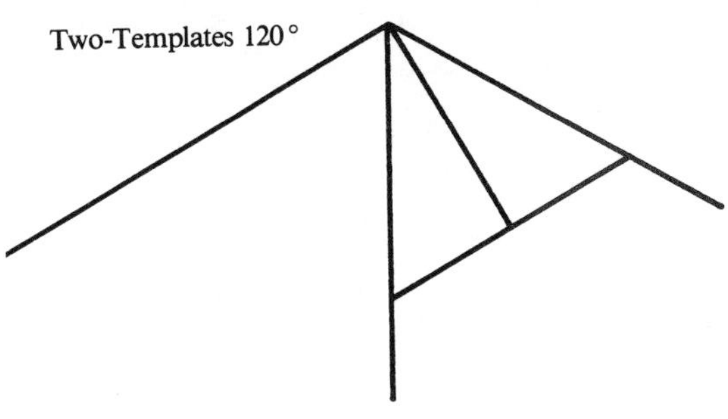

The One-Template Angle

Many of these shapes include a 60° angle. This is one template. You may draw this on paper, making a pattern, or you may use a marking pen or pencil on your fabric.

The Two-Template Angle

To obtain a 120° angle, draw two sides of one template. Pick up the template and position it along the outside of the second line. Draw the new outside line.

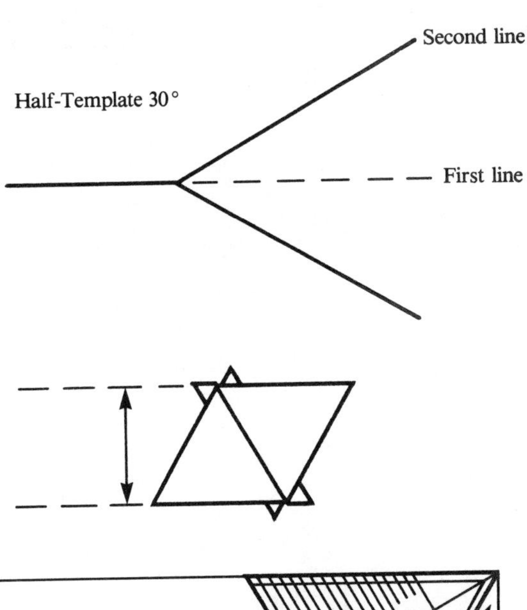

The Half-Template

To obtain a 30° angle, draw a line. Place the perpendicular of your template on this line. Draw one side of your template. Extend these sidelines as necessary, using a transparent ruler.

Diamond Shapes

You can quickly cut 60° diamonds to any size you need. Measure the diamond you need from parallel side to parallel side. (You can find the diamond by sewing two of your triangles together and pressing this flat; a diamond made from two 4" triangles measures 3-3/4" across the width.) Cut strips from fabric to this width (3-3/4" strips for a diamond to be sewn onto 4" triangles). Layer, press, and cut up to 8 strips at a time.

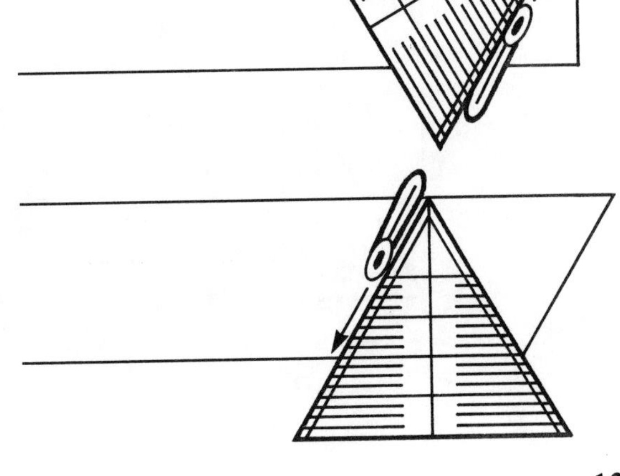

1. Place your template with one long side along one edge of your strip. Cut the end of the strip to a one-template angle.
2. Move the template, putting the base line right at the edge of the cut you just made, lining it up with the strip edge. Cut along the side opposite the first cut. Keep moving the template to the edge of the angle and cutting the opposite side, producing diamonds until you run out of strip.

TECHNIQUES

STRIP–PIECING

Symmetrical — Same on both sides

Repeat
(Can be Symmetrical or Asymmetrical)

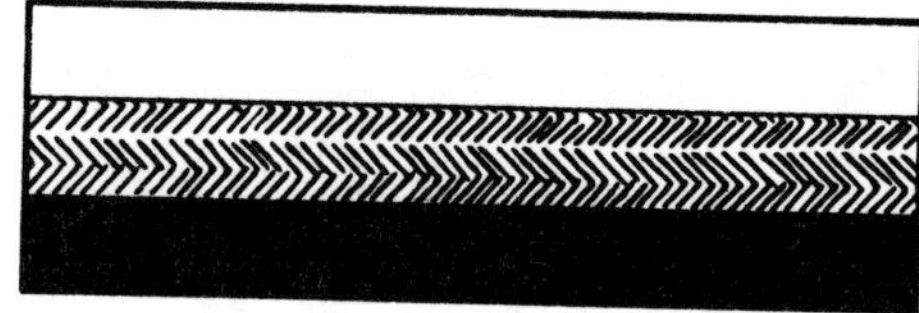

Shaded

Unique

Strata: set of strips

There are four kinds of strata to construct for these designs: symmetrical, repeat, shaded, and unique. It helps if you can plan a symmetrical strata because you quickly get many pieces with little waste.

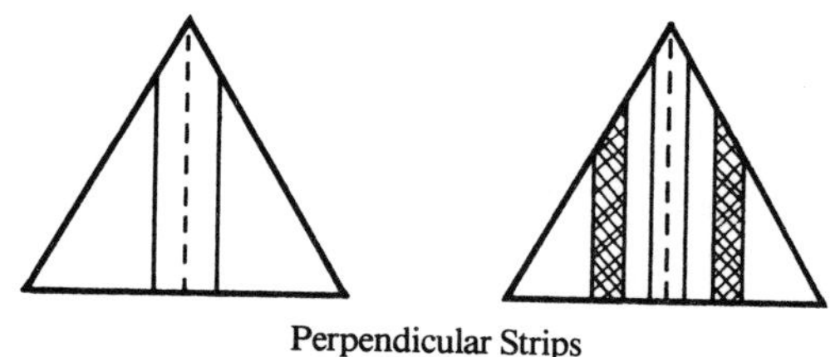

Perpendicular Strips

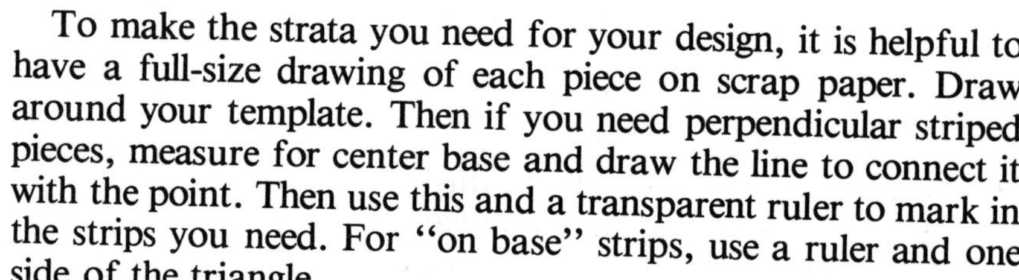

To make the strata you need for your design, it is helpful to have a full-size drawing of each piece on scrap paper. Draw around your template. Then if you need perpendicular striped pieces, measure for center base and draw the line to connect it with the point. Then use this and a transparent ruler to mark in the strips you need. For "on base" strips, use a ruler and one side of the triangle.

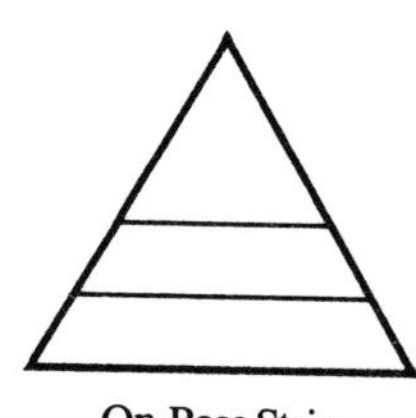

On Base Strip

Check to make sure that you don't have disappearing triangles in the corners. Seam allowances take up quite a bit more than you think and triangles in the points need to be quite substantial to make any visual impact. So, for example, you might consider changing from equally divided strata to wider strips on the edges and slightly narrower strips in the center, or for some "on base" triangles, plan to use a much wider strip on the outside points.

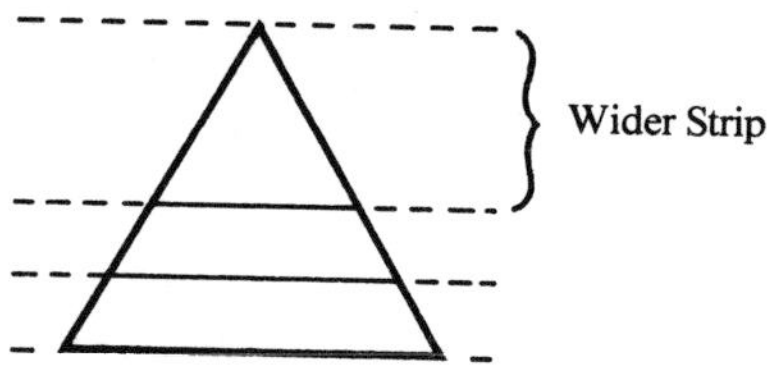

Wider Strip

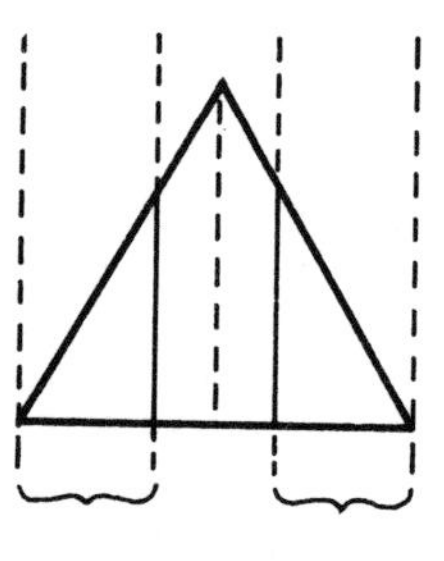

Wider Strip

In all cases these rules hold:

1. All strip widths need to have seam allowances of 1/4'' on each side (1/2'' total) added to them, except outside strips of a strata need only one 1/4'' seam allowance added. Templates include seam allowance.

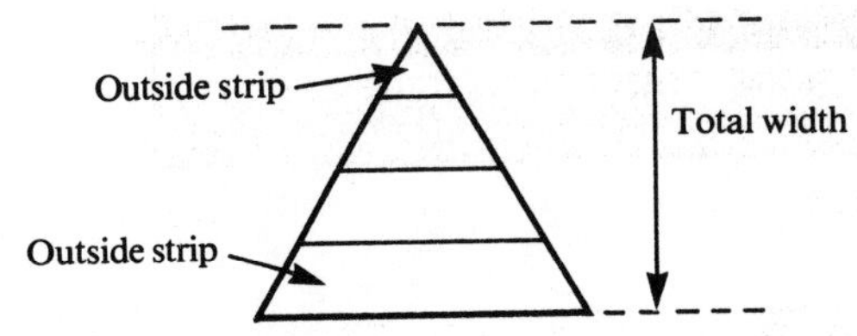

2. Total width of a strata must be:

   For perpendicular striped triangles: The measurement of the base plus seam allowance (same as the base on your template).

   For parallel striped triangles: The height of the perpendicular plus seam allowance (same as the perpendicular on your template).

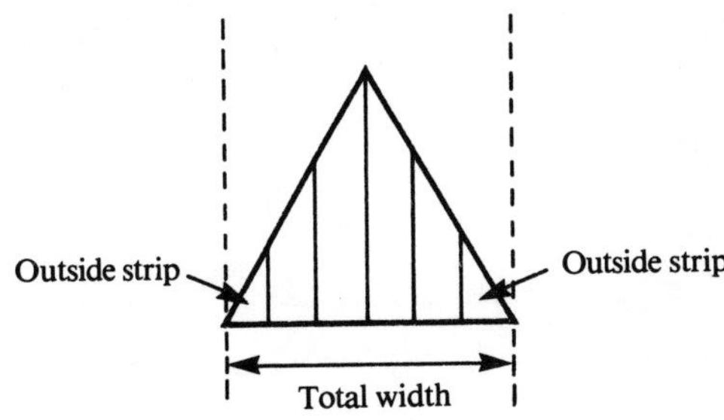

To determine fabric requirements, you can calculate the amount of each color needed from:

- The width of a color strip
- The number of triangles using this color and the measurement of your base including seam allowance
- A bit extra for waste

For example:

Using preshrunk fabric, 45'' wide, and making color strip 2'' wide (including seams), you need 12 triangles with a base measurement of 4-3/4''.

45'' ÷ 4-3/4'' = 9 triangles per strip, so you only need two strips or 4'' of 45'' wide material. The minimum to purchase would be 6'' to make sure you are cutting on straight of grain and to allow for cutting mistakes.

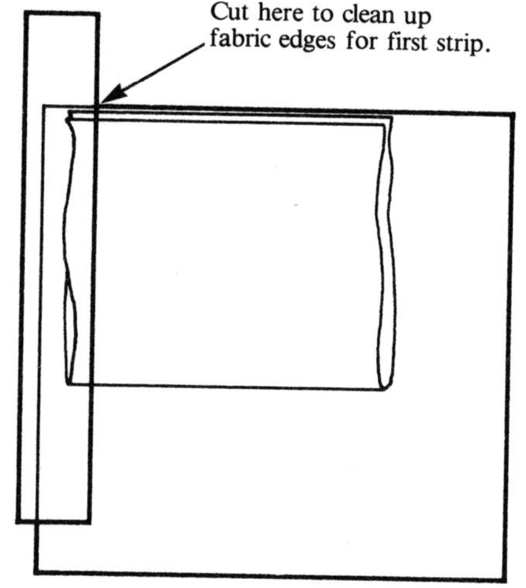

Oops!

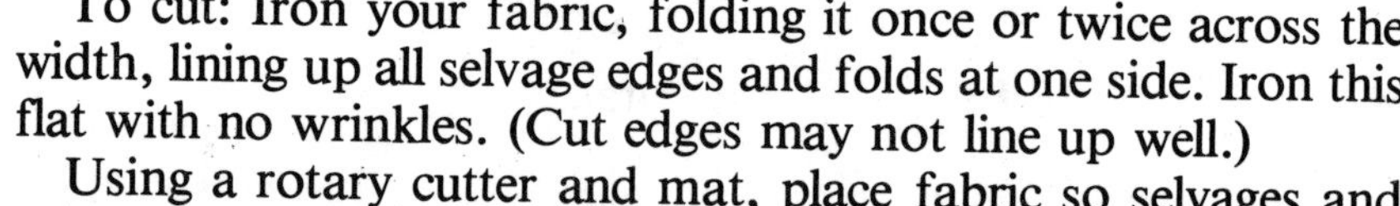

To cut: Iron your fabric, folding it once or twice across the width, lining up all selvage edges and folds at one side. Iron this flat with no wrinkles. (Cut edges may not line up well.)

Using a rotary cutter and mat, place fabric so selvages and folds are at the bottom or top edge of your mat. Line transparent ruler up with side of mat and cut along it to clean edge for first strip. Check also for straight of grain, but you may have to vary from it due to fabric printing. Work as close to the straight grain as possible.

Cut the first strip and open it up to be sure it's not a zig-zag. If it is straight, cut the rest of your strips. If it is not straight, check again to be sure the selvages are together and lined up with the edge of the mat, and the folded fabric is flat and has no wrinkles. It always works for me. You may also cut these strips with sharp scissors, using a table edge to align the selvages and marking the lines with a pencil and ruler. If you don't have a scissors that can handle four layers of fabric without distortion, you can mark the strip for the whole length.

Seam the strips together holding both tightly and pulling slightly to prevent the feed dog from easing in more of the bottom fabric, which will distort the strata.

Sew all the strips together in order and then press flat, pulling across the width of the strata to make sure there's no fabric lost in a fold. Press all the seams in one direction. I press from the back first and then from the front. I always use a dry iron, keeping a wet press cloth handy, just in case.

To cut "on base" triangles, lay the strata with one end toward you. (You may try cutting two sets of strips at a time, if you wish.) Always keep the triangle base along the same side of the strata as you cut. Each time you move your template for the next cuts, line up the two triangle base points exactly, and the opposite triangles will still be accurate.

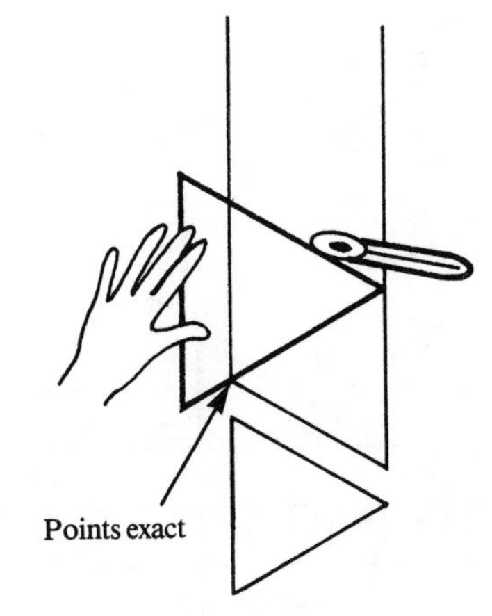

Some designs made from "on base" triangles only use one side of a strata. It's a waste to throw half of your fabric away (even though you're saving time). If you cut all of your pieces accurately, the waste pieces usually can be arranged in a separate design. An example is In the Clover which was made from the waste pieces of Night Sky. Interesting quilts have been made by those challenged to use these waste pieces. Or, if you are working on a design, be aware of this and include both sides of the strata in your design, as in Rose's Star.

Strata #2 from Rose's Star

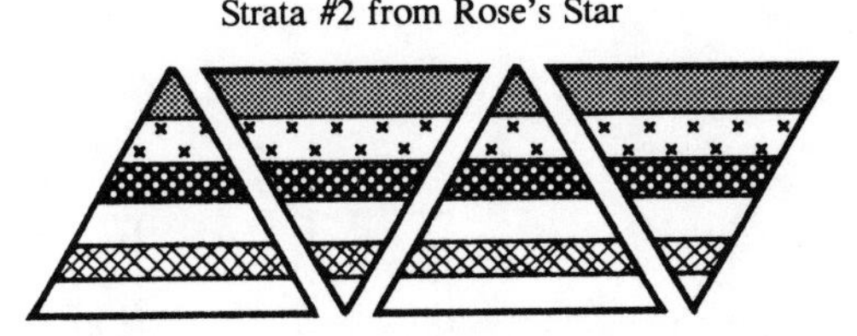

When cutting a perpendicular stripe, a little more work is required. Use the perpendicular center line of your template to line it up on the strata. Leave at least 1/4" between the top points of your triangles; bottoms can be tight together.

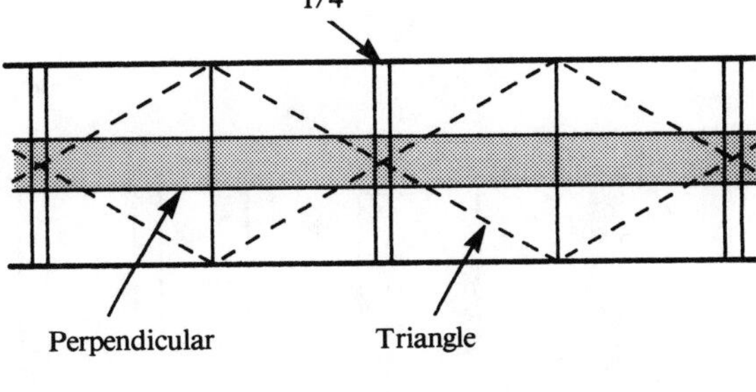

Your waste pieces will look like this. You can seam these pieces to a center strip and get more perpendicular triangles.

The pairs of waste triangles must be lined up very carefully and be at least 1/2" apart. Depending on the color arrangement of the original strata, you may get triangles exactly like your originals or the reverse arrangment, or something quite different, especially if you use a different color down the center stripe.

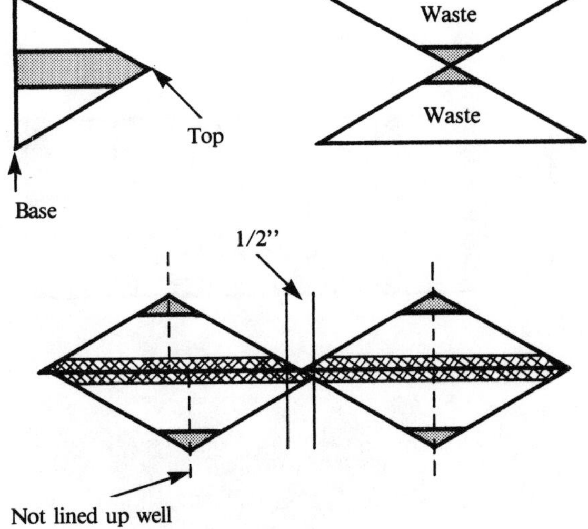

They must be lined up very carefully and be at least ½" apart.

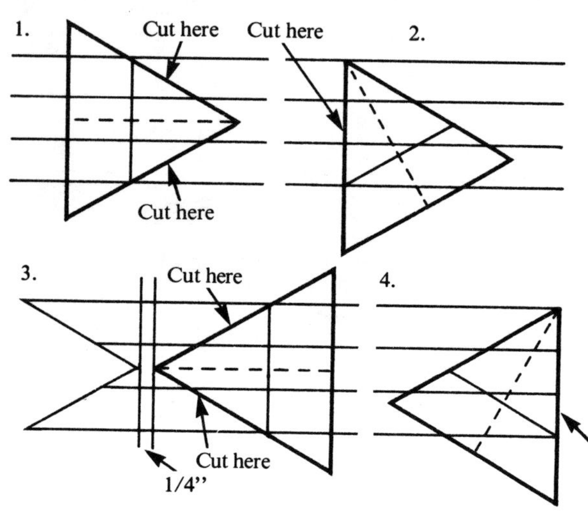

If you are cutting one of the smaller triangles on your template from a perpendicular stripe strata, you cut your triangles in this fashion: Cut the two long sides first. Then pick up the template and turn it so one of the fabric cuts lines up with your base line and the other with a long side. Then cut along the other long side to complete the triangle.

Line up your template again for the second triangle (1/4" away) and cut the two long sides. Pick up the template and turn it, so the chosen base line is along one cut line and a long side along another cut line, and cut the third edge to complete the triangle.

Example: The Sail from Sailboats and Icebergs

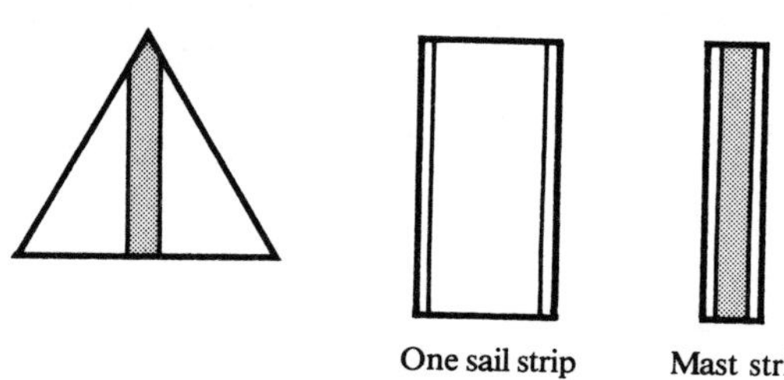

To avoid waste in designs made from perpendicular triangles, try planning your strip-piecing in two steps. This only works for some strata.

First, make half the strata you need for your triangle, including the whole center strip. Add seam allowances on both sides of all strips.

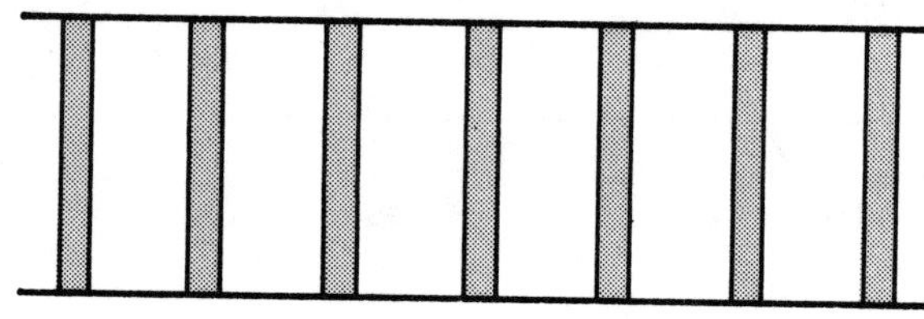

Take the half-strata and cut this into pieces as long as the height of your triangle, plus 1/4". Seam these pieces together to make a continuous strip of repeats.

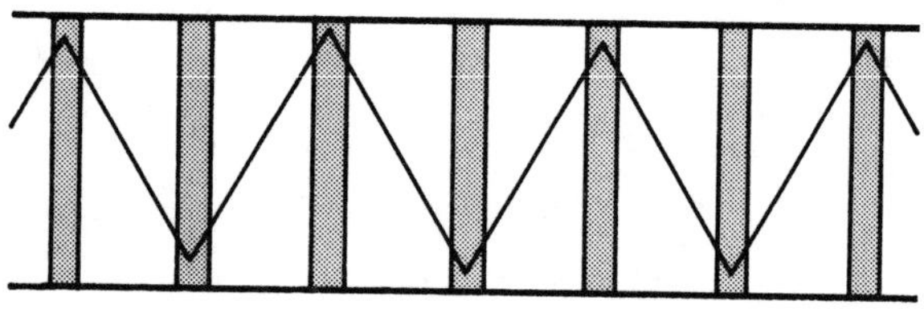

Second, cut your triangles, using your perpendicular as your guide.

SANDWICH-PIECING

When using this method, you work with two pieces of fabric at the same time, laying right sides together. You mark and sew, so that when you finally cut, you already have done the piecing.

Notice that all sewing is done on straight of grain. This will minimize fabric distortion. Work with fabric scraps first, until you get it right.

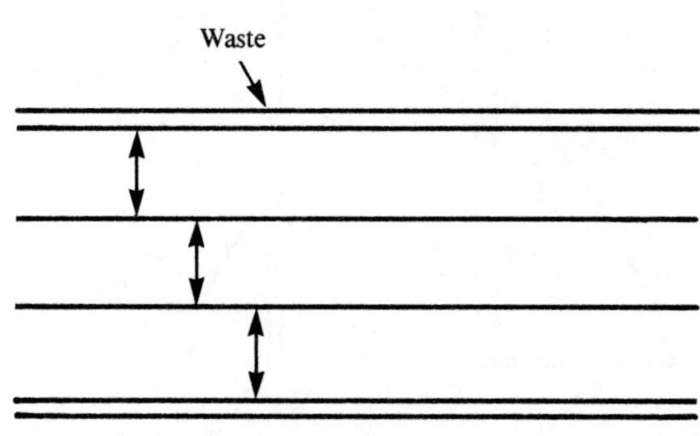

Matching Triangles: This technique produces very little waste. Lay light and dark fabrics right sides together, matching edge(s). Press them both together. On light fabric on the wrong side, mark strips across the fabric, using the measurement of the height of your triangle's perpendicular. Mark with pencil. Angle your marker toward the ruler for greater accuracy. Use your template to carefully mark triangles along the lines. It should look like the diagram for matching triangles.

Diagram for Matching Triangles

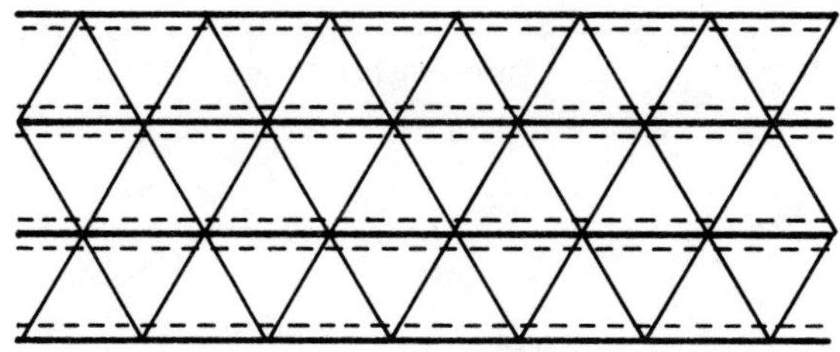

Seam through both materials on each side of the base lines 1/4" away. Press flat again. Then cut apart on all drawn lines.

To sandwich-piece small amounts of matching triangles: Cut strips the width of your triangle's perpendicular (4" strips if you are working with 4" triangles). Seam two strips (one light, one dark) right sides together. First seam them together down one side with a 1/4" seam. Then seam down the other side. Press this to reduce distortion. Using your template and a rotary cutter, cut triangles from this strip. Pull the matching pairs apart at the tip and press open.

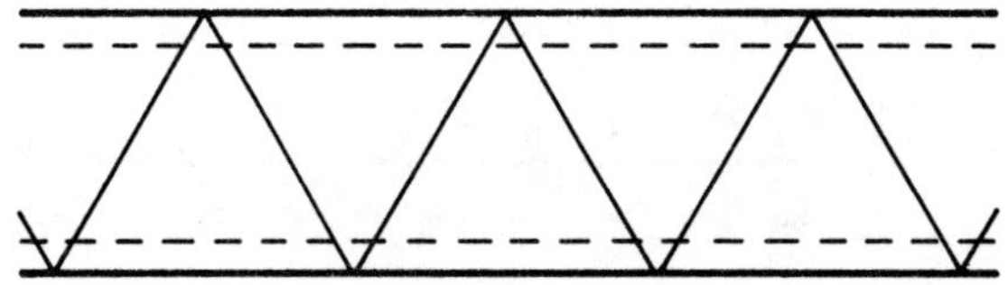

Finished Matching Triangles

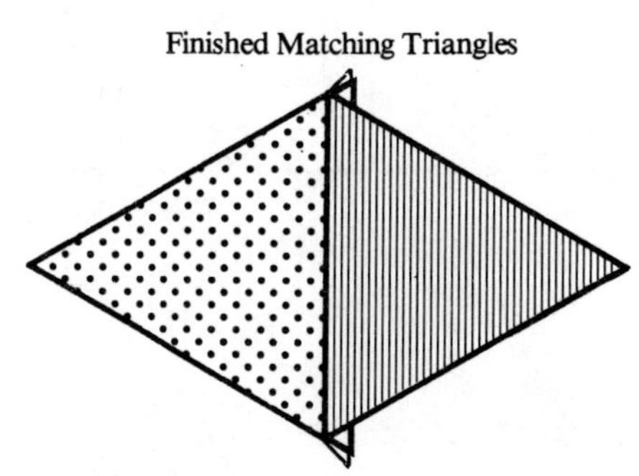

Half-Triangles: You will need to make a paper pattern of the half-triangle in the size you desire. This includes the added seam allowance and will be used instead of the markings on your template.

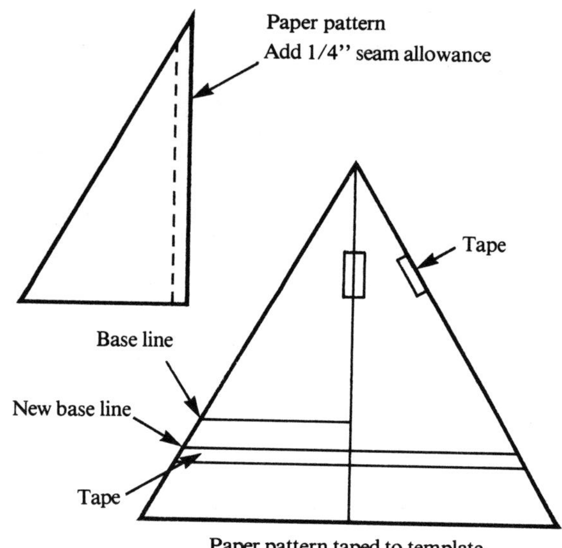

Paper pattern taped to template

Draw the length of one side to your triangle's base. Mark the top and bottom of the perpendicular. Mark where your triangle's base intersects the left and right side. Remove the template and using the marks, draw the half-triangle's base line and perpendicular. With a transparent ruler, add 1/4" seam allowance to the perpendicular. Extend the base and side line of the half-triangle to meet the new perpendicular. This is the paper pattern of your half-triangle.

Cut out this paper pattern and tape it to your template at the side and along the perpendicular. The paper pattern base line will extend farther than the measurement of your finished triangle because of the added seam allowance. Stick a piece of transparent tape all the way across your template to mark this new base line. Check with a ruler to make sure it's parallel with the template base (bottom edge). (If you are using a finished triangle the size of this template make a larger template.)

Diagram for Half-Triangles

Seam either side of vertical line 1/4" away.

Lay the light and dark fabrics right sides together, matching edge(s). Press them both together. Then, on the wrong side of the light fabric, mark lines across the fabric the height of your new perpendicular. With your template, use the new base line to mark triangles along the lines, as for matching triangles. Draw a perpendicular line connecting all the top points of your triangles. (It should look like the diagram for half-triangles.) Seam through both materials on each side of the vertical lines 1/4" away. Press perfectly flat again, then cut apart on all drawn lines.

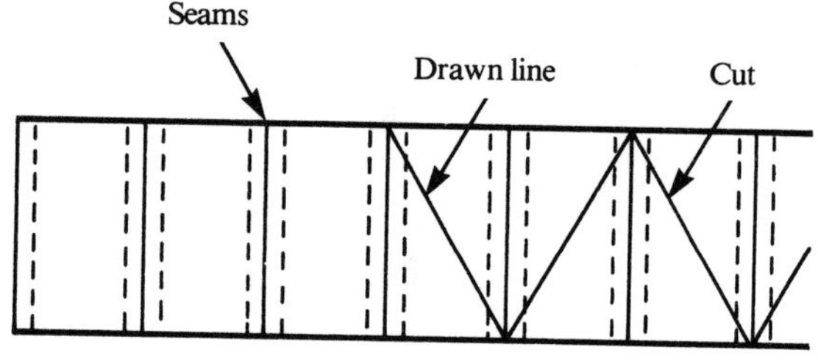

After cutting along the lines and pressing your half-triangles, you will have both right- and left-handed units. Either design your quilt so you use both or save the units you don't need for another piece.

Finished Half-Triangles

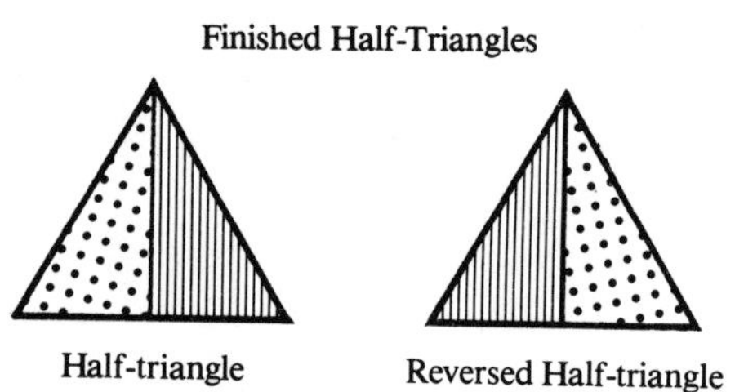

Half-triangles also can be sandwich-pieced in small amounts. When you have drawn the paper pattern for your half-triangle, measure the new perpendicular height to use for the strip width (4-1/2" for a 4" half-triangle). Lay your dark and light strips right sides together. Measure your new base line. Mark lines across the top strip as far apart as half of the new base. Seam across the strips 1/4" away on both sides of every line. Then place your template with the perpendicular line over every other line across your strips and use a rotary cutter to cut out triangles. Cut the center lines and press your half-triangles open.

Rose's Star, 49¾" x 55", uses both sides of two strata. The pastel colors create a storybook effect. It is based on a design by Rose Herrera, Snohomish, Washington, who made a similar baby quilt for her granddaughter.

Viola, 54¾" x 68½", is a brand-new pattern with the appeal of a traditional design. The pansies climb a trellis quilted with vines, for a charming garden effect.

Sailboats and Icebergs, 48" x 57½", done in nautical colors, feels like it's tossing on the waves. Select graphic prints to carry out the theme.

Snowbound Star, 33" x 61", Donna Endresen, 1986, Poulsbo, Washington. This banner has a Scandinavian flavor and would add a welcoming touch to an entry hall.

Snowstorm, 54¼" x 66½", uses many different prints to overwhelm the eye with snow. This is a sampler quilt of triangle designs.

Wind Farm, 60" x 72", an original design by Rebecca Rudd, 1986, Arlington, Washington. This sampler of blue windmills looks like it could produce enough energy for a small town.

Spider Web, 51" x 70", is a lovely old-fashioned design. When executed as a scrap quilt, it is easy to assemble.

Atomic Structure, 65" x 70", a version of the Spider Web design laid out with complete webs of color, creating a modern effect. Triangular shadows play across the quilt.

Night Sky, 30" x 45", a speed-pieced hexagon design, has floating constellations and galaxies behind the bright star points.

In The Clover, 45" x 45", is made from the waste pieces of Night Sky.

Razzle Dazzle, 73½" x 91", has a cut-glass effect. The diamond-shaped blocks are arranged in a baby-block pattern according to color and value.

Shooting Stars, 71½" x 101", done in multi-colored solid fabrics, looks like a stop-action photograph of fast moving stars.

Gold Star, 45½" x 56¼", looks like a garden viewed through a cut-glass window. Done in two colors, it resembles an old-fashioned classic quilt.

Peaks in Sunshine, 28" x 32½", an original design made by Vera Parrish, 1986, Bellingham, Washington. This simple design has many possibilities. Done in bright colors it has an art deco feel.

Granny Square, 61¾" x 91¼", uses both types of half-triangles and can be constructed from scraps. The border of this quilt extends the design past its own boundaries. Another border could be added as a frame.

Wreath, 73" x 82", an original design made by Florence Pekola, 1986, Lake Stevens, Washington. This easy and economical red and green design makes an effective Christmas quilt. It is finished with machine quilting.

Peacock Snowflake, 34½" x 41", an original design made by Reynola Pakusik, 1986, Bellingham, Washington. One beautiful snowflake makes a hexagonal wall hanging.

The Half-Diamond

The half-diamond is another kind of matching triangle based on the equilateral triangle.

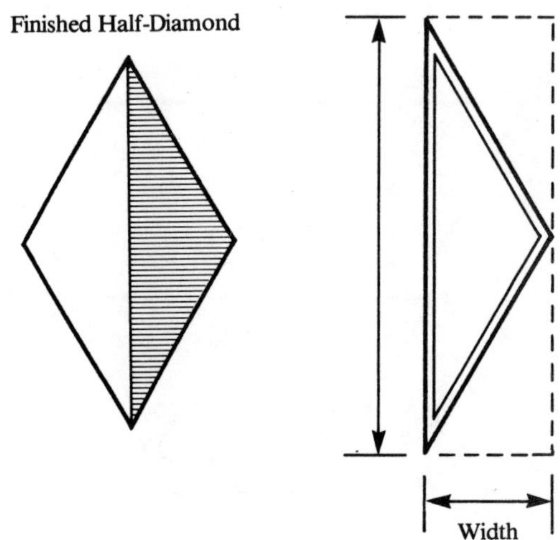

You will need to make a paper pattern of a half-diamond: (Always use a fine-tipped pen or sharp pencil and slant it toward the ruler.)

1. Using the plastic template, draw your triangle.
2. Mark and draw the perpendicular line, extending it below your triangle at least the distance of your triangle's perpendicular.
3. Reverse the plastic template. Line it up along the extended perpendicular line, with the base line of the drawn triangle exactly under the same line less 1/2" on the plastic template. (3-1/2" for a 4" triangle)
4. Draw one side.
5. Add 1/4" seam allowance to the perpendicular line, extending sides to meet this.

Base line
1/2"
Base line
Perpendicular
Perpendicular with seam allowance

This is your pattern for a half-diamond. You may glue this to thin cardboard, cutting away the excess with a mat knife or rolling cutter along a transparent ruler. Now you have your template for a half-diamond.

Diagram for Half-Diamonds

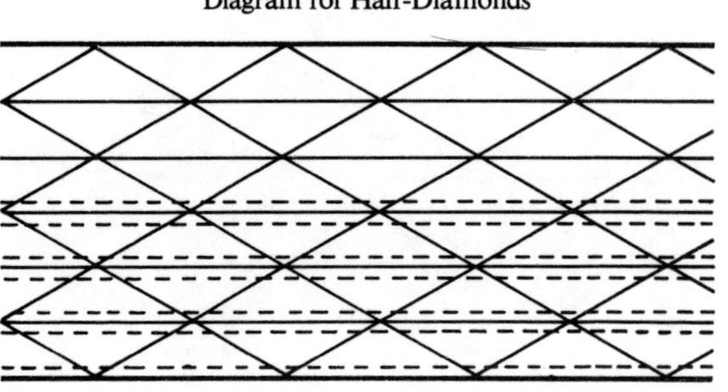

Lay the light and dark fabrics right sides together, matching edge(s). Press them both together. Then, on the wrong side of your light fabric, mark lines across the fabric the width of your half-diamond. With your template, using the length of the perpendicular along the lines, mark triangles along the horizontal lines. The diagonal lines should connect, forming a grid.

Seam through both materials on each side of the base line 1/4" away. Press. Then cut apart on all drawn lines.

QUILT CONSTRUCTION

Triangles

Another straight line

Certain methods of sewing these triangles together are easier than others. Any shape that allows you to sew continuous straight lines is preferred.

If you must make a hexagon, add points to it to make it a diamond. You may need to borrow parts of an adjacent star or hexagon to do this. A diamond is a good continuous unit for these designs. In fact, it might be called the "basic square" for equilateral triangles. To sew these designs easily, it is often best to have all the triangles constructed and laid out in your pattern.

When you start sewing these pieces, you may have a little trouble matching seams, since they come together at unfamiliar angles. Take it out and do it over, and soon you will be familiar with the appearance of the seams. It may help you to pin the seams and open them to see how you're doing. Depending on your quilting pattern, you may choose to press some row seams open to reduce bulk.

When constructing any quilt top from your design, choose which size of triangle you want to work with. Seams take up 3/4" of the perpendicular measurement and 7/8" across the base. So a triangle that has a 4" perpendicular and a 4-5/8" base becomes 3-1/4" x 3-3/4" finished size.

Seams often look like this

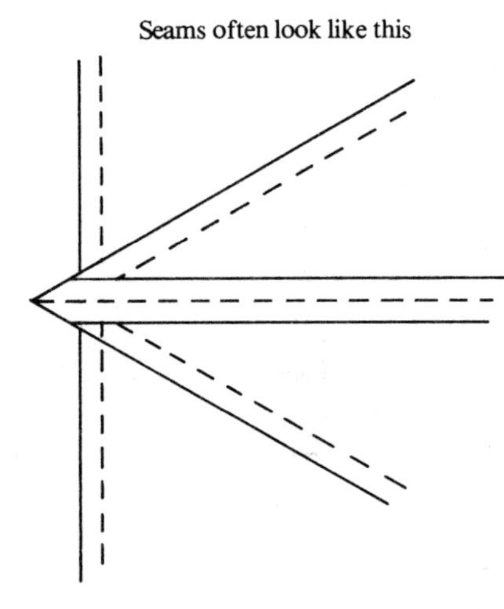

A little math will reveal the size of the finished top. For example, the Viola quilt pattern given in the back of this book has 16 perpendiculars down the length of the top (not including borders). Use of a triangle template with a 4" perpendicular results in a top approximately 52" in length and 41-1/4" in width without borders. Substituting a larger triangle template changes the measurements accordingly.

Whatever triangle you choose, in most cases you must then use this template for the construction of the whole quilt. You would use it to design and cut strata, half-triangles, matching triangles, half-diamonds, or even plain triangles. These would all then fit together accurately to make your top. (If you want to combine various template sizes, fine. Begin by taping together various sections of the two sizes of graph paper given or glue them onto a background.)

Bias seams should not cause problems with your piecing. Do not worry, they do not require special attention. You will become familiar with what the intersections should look like as you continue piecing, and then you may want to stretch a piece here and there to get a perfect fit. Bias helps!

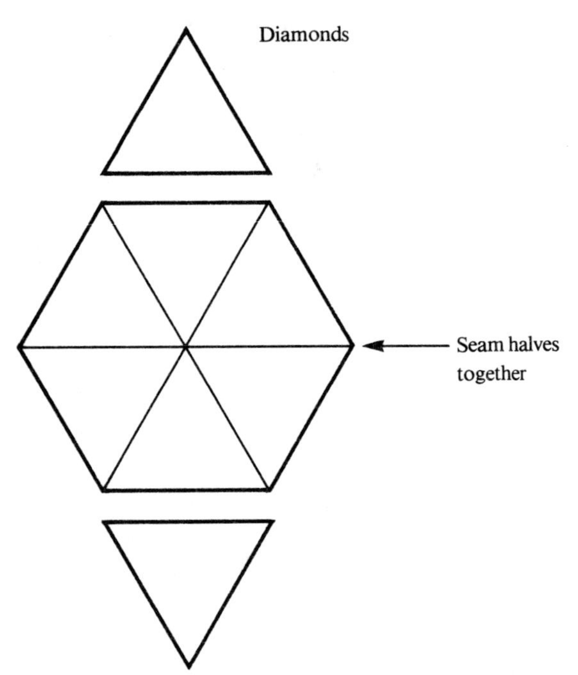

In the process of constructing your quilt top, it is better to save the seaming of the quilt top until last. In many cases, you won't even construct blocks, but will lay out your various triangles until you can see the whole top. A pre-colored design on graph paper can help you avoid mistakes. It is more difficult to remove parts and substitute others after your top is partially sewn together than when you have all the elements laid out on the floor and are looking at it with your best critical judgment. It is also more difficult to set in a star or hexagon than it is to sew rows of parallel seams. (But with practice, it can be done. I know!)

Use a large table top or part of the floor if you don't have a design wall you can get some distance from. Lay it out and then squint while you evaluate colors and forms. (Laying it out and picking it up can be part of an exercise program—and good quilts are one result!) Then the easiest way to sew it together is often into diamonds, then into parallel rows, into larger diamonds, and then into parallel rows of panels.

Rows and panels

FINISHED EDGES

Most of these designs automatically have two straight sides and two angular sides. You may decide to bind the angular edges as they are, as a kind of fancy finishing touch. Or you may want to straighten the edges to have four straight sides, in order to add borders or for ease of binding. Each design may suggest the most effective way to finish the edge.

If you wish to add plain borders, it is often best to measure your top across the center horizontally and vertically, to avoid bias stretch on the edges.

Additional pattern pieces

Additional Pattern Pieces

Plan pieces that will fill in the ends of each row and complete the design. Add these before sewing the rows together. After the top is all pieced, trim the edge to a straight line, if desired.

Rough Fill-In Pieces

Cut a strip of background fabric the width of your row plus seam allowances. Trim just one end of this strip at the proper angle (use your template) and seam it to the end of a row. Press flat. Measure a length on this added strip. Allow more than is needed to line up with the next row. Cut off the rest of the strip. Trim this to the proper angle again and add it to the end of another row. Continue until all the row ends have the extra fabric added. Then seam all the rows together. Press. Trim edge of top carefully with rotary cutter or scissors.

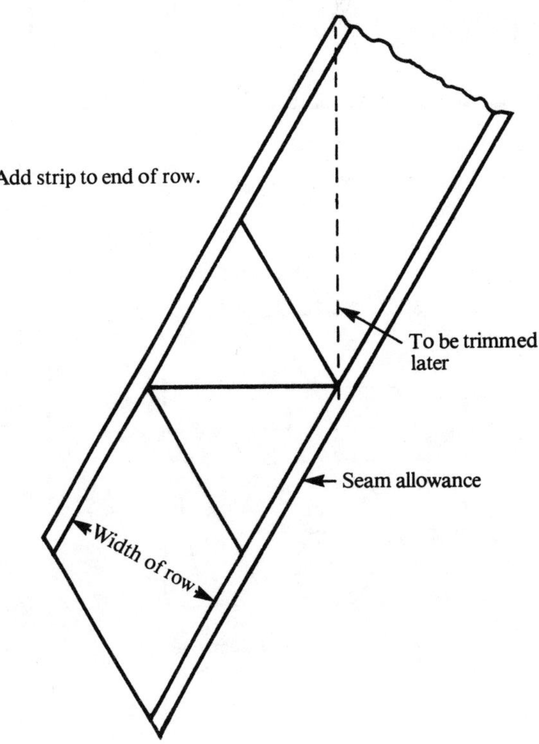

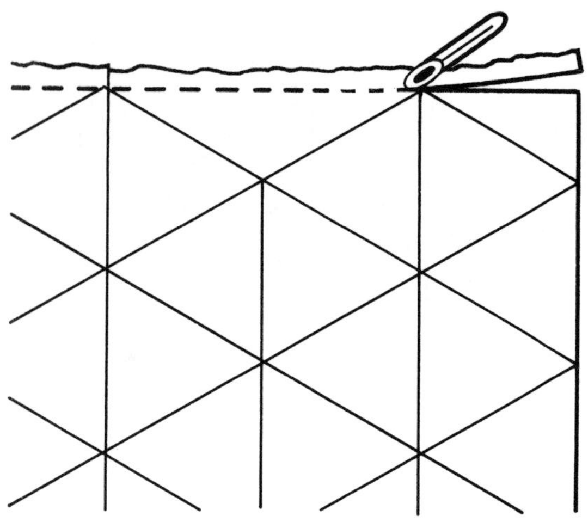

When the design will allow it, use blocks with plain pieces and simply cut off the excess to straighten the edge. Often it will improve or complete your design to also use partial blocks (or plain pieces cut to the proper angles) to finish your top.

Other tops are easy to finish. If you complete your design well within the borders of the quilt, your final shape will easily become a natural rectangle.

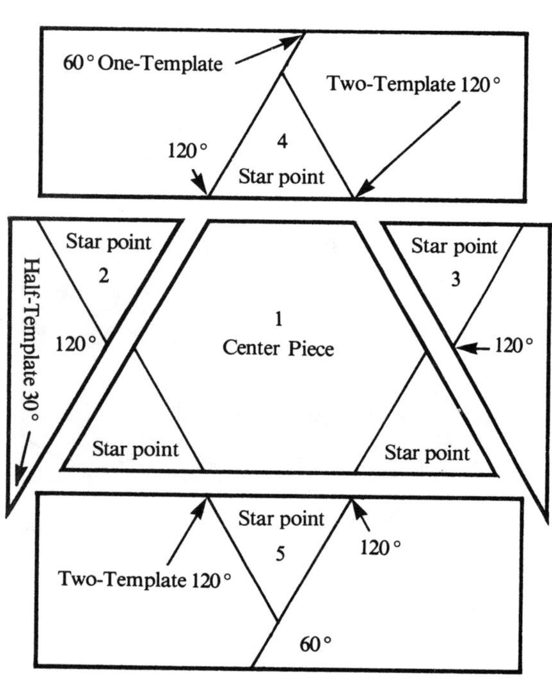

A star is assembled in five sections. The center piece has two star points on it. All the other sections consist of a star point with background pieces added. Find the proper angles quickly with your template and cut the piece a bit larger than you need. When the star is together, trim the edges to a rectangle, staying 1/2" to 1" away from the star points. Add borders as desired. Remember, you can recognize the angle at a glance. One-template, two-template, or half-template angles are easy to identify, and that is all you need to work with.

Hexagons and diamonds become rectangles with the addition of four corner pieces.

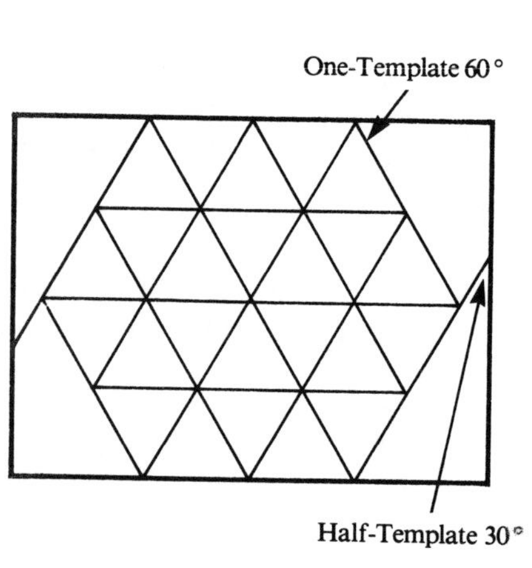

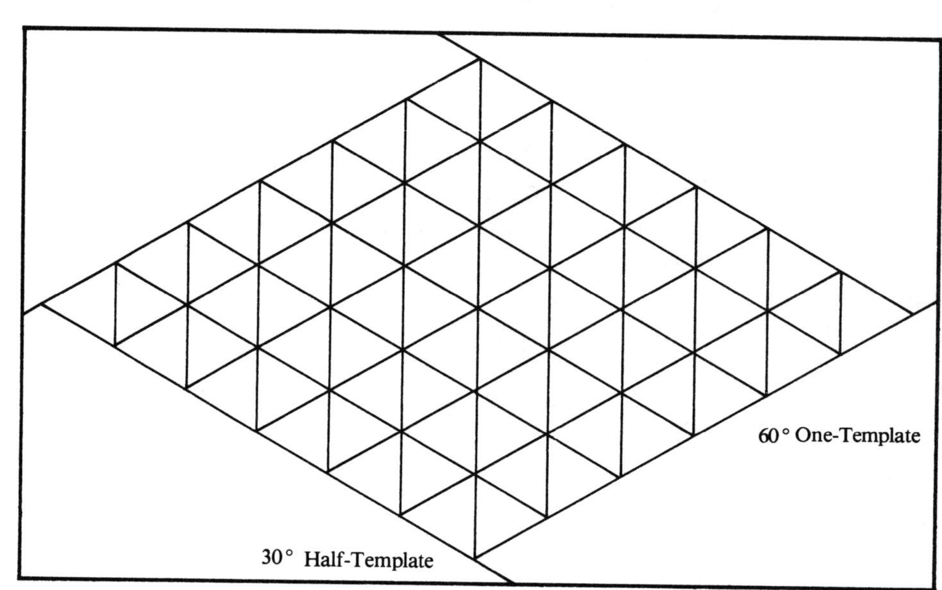

PATTERNS

All eleven quilt patterns and directions are given in the same format. Listed first is the name of the piecing technique used to produce the design followed by the size of the triangle template used for cutting. Triangle size is the perpendicular measurement of the triangle.

Example: Strip-piecing; on base
Triangle Size: 6''

If this quilt is cut from strata, a little symbolic strata is drawn with the width given for each strip. Seam allowances are always included and sewing these strips together will result in the width of strata needed for the size triangle you are using. Take an accurate 1/4'' seam allowance.

Example:

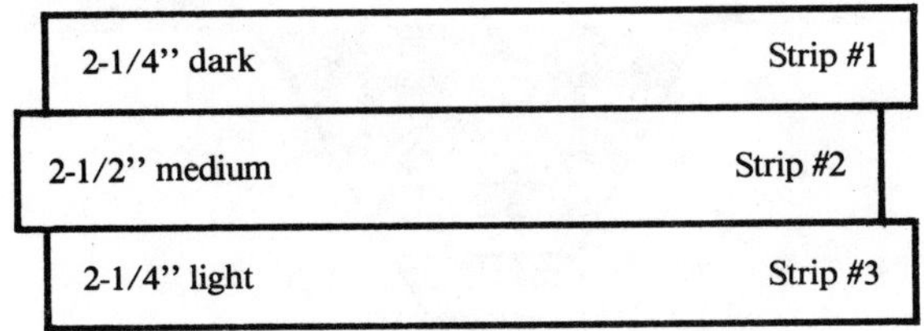

Adds up to 7'' but after piecing equals 6''.

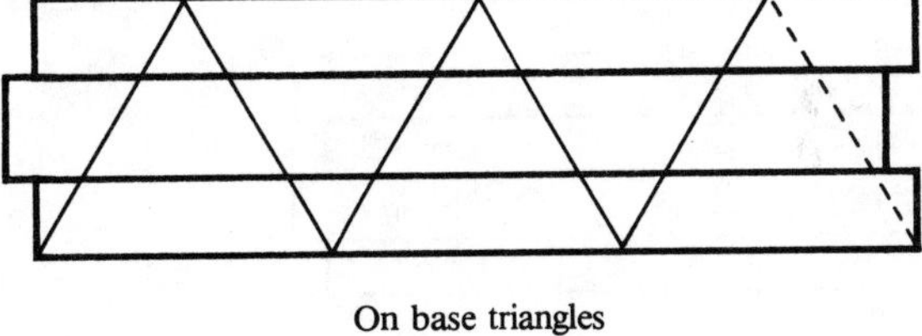

On base triangles

Next, if a repeat block is used, a drawing is given so you can see how to assemble one unit.

Fabric requirements, based on 44-45'' wide fabric, are planned to allow for shrinkage. Color choices or suggestions are indicated. You may choose to duplicate the colors in the projects shown, or substitute your favorite colors.

Last are step-by-step directions for the assembly of each top. You may need to refer back in the book if you cannot recall a particular technique. If you have trouble seeing one row or section, lay one or two pieces of paper over the illustration until your eye finds the assembly order.

Note: the patterns at the beginning tend to be easiest and the patterns near the end of the section a bit more difficult. The first seven patterns use strip-piecing and the last four patterns use sandwich-piecing. They are all fast.

Have fun making whichever quilt you choose!

ROSE'S STAR

Strip-piecing: on base
Triangle Size: 6"
Design Size: 42" x 36-3/4"
Strata: 6" wide

Construct 3 of each strata

#1 Strata (includes seam allowances):
Cut 24 triangles from:

2-1/4" dark	Strip #1
2-1/2" medium	Strip #2
2-1/4" light	Strip #3

Makes a 6" strata

#2 Strata (includes seam allowances):
Cut triangles from:

1-1/2"	Strip #1
1-1/4"	Strip #2
1-1/2"	Strip #3
1-1/4"	Strip #4
1-1/2"	Strip #5
1-1/2"	Strip #6

Makes a 6" strata

Use 3 colors used in Strata #1 plus 3 more colors.

Fabric requirements (from preshrunk fabric at least 43" wide):

- 1/3 - 1/2 yd. of 3 major colors
- 1/6 - 1/4 yd. of 3 accent colors
- 1 yd. of background fabric

(pictured on page 21)

Directions:

Construct strata. Press. Using your 6" template, cut triangles on base. Arrange 6 triangles in center. Finish arranging star. Cut background pieces to the proper size and angle. All fill-in pieces are made with a two-template angle (120°). Measure edges of star to determine measurement. Using angle patterns and diagram on page 32, piece the fill-in pieces with a star point in each unit and sew them with a straight seam.

SPIDER WEB

Strip-piecing: on base
Triangle Size: 5''
Design Size: 51'' x 70''

Strata: 5'' wide

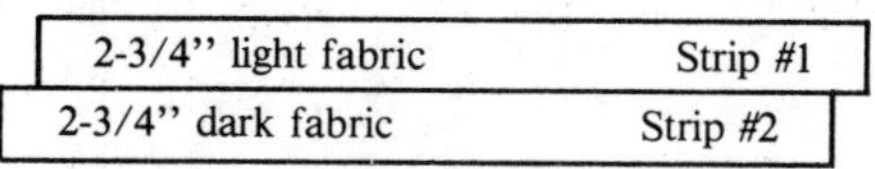

One block

Half block

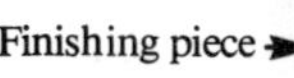

(pictured on page 24)

Spider Web Block

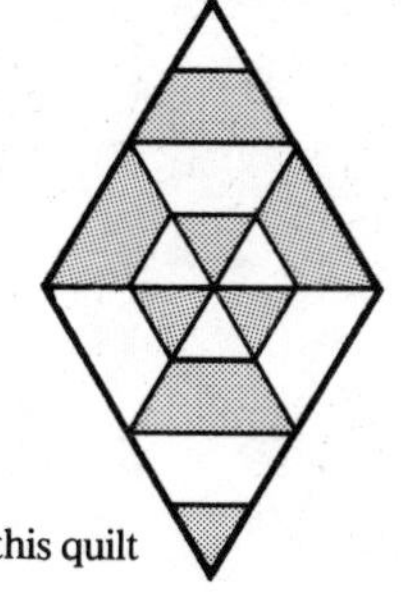

24 needed in this quilt

Dark-Tipped Half Block

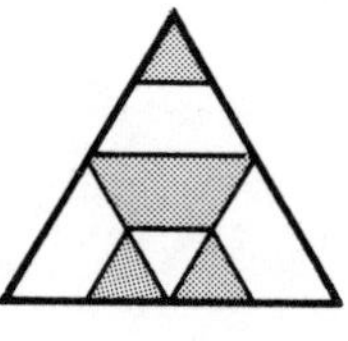

15 needed in this quilt

Light-Tipped Half Block

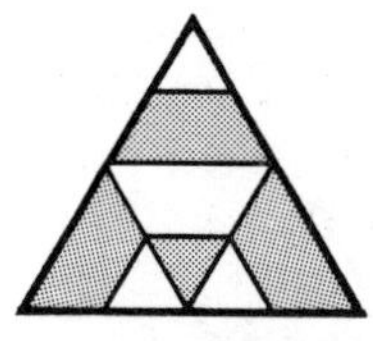

15 needed in this quilt

Finishing Pieces

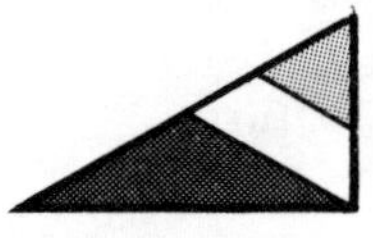

6 needed in this quilt

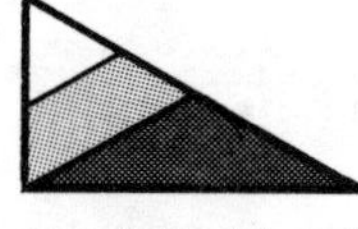

6 needed in this quilt

Fabric Requirements:

2-1/2 yds. light fabrics
2-1/2 yds. dark fabrics

Directions:

Construct strata. Make your strata from leftover dark and light fabrics you have, or try a 2-color quilt. (Example: blue and white.) Using 5'' template, cut triangles on base from strata. Sew 4 blocks and 5 half blocks alternately into each row. Finish each row with the proper finishing piece. Sew the rows together. Add borders if desired.

Try an alternate assembly as used in the ''Atomic Structure'' quilt shown on page 24. Lay the triangles out in rows or panels without sewing them into blocks first. Coordinate the colors of the half blocks. This requires a little more space and time but gives you more control over the colors of the spider web.

VIOLA

Strip-piecing: on base
Triangle Size: 4"
Design Size: 54-3/4" x 68-1/2" with borders

(pictured on page 21)

Strata: 4" wide

#1 Strata (includes seam allowances):

Fabric	Strip
1-1/4" green solid	Strip #1
3-1/4" muslin	Strip #2

#2 Strata (includes seam allowances):

Fabric	Strip
1-3/4" assorted blue, purple, mauve	Strip #1
1-1/4" black or other color	Strip #2
2" yellow print or solid	Strip #3

#3 Strata (includes seam allowances):

Fabric	Strip
1-3/4" assorted blue, purple, mauve	Strip #1
2-3/4" muslin	Strip #2

Viola Block

18 needed

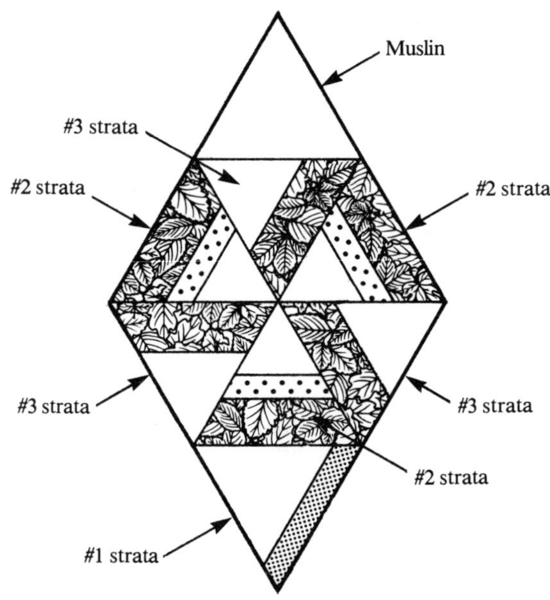

Fabric Requirements:

1/8 yd. green solid
2/3 - 1 yd. of mixed blue, purple, mauve
1/4 yd. black and/or other color
1/2 yd. yellow print or solid
2-3/4 yds. muslin
Borders require extra fabric.

After constructing the blocks for this quilt, you will have some waste triangles, possibly enough for a small wall hanging or lap quilt.

Cutting Specifications

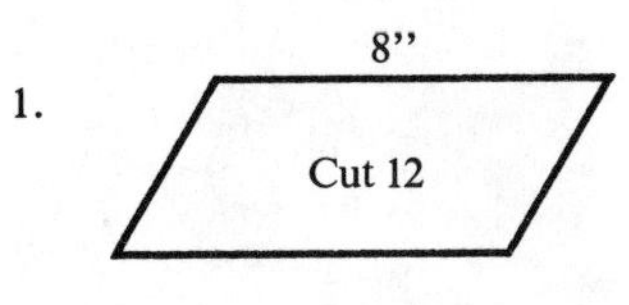

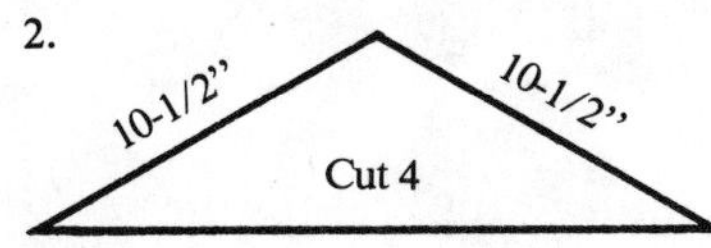

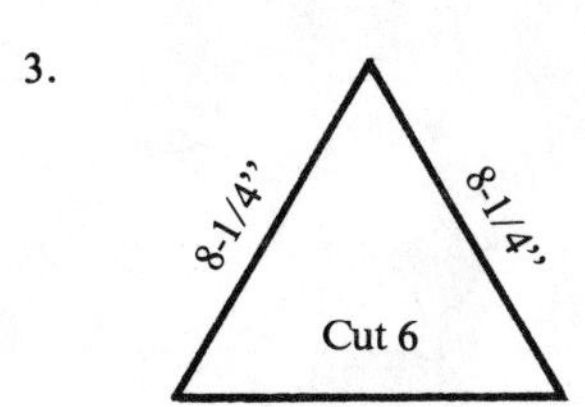

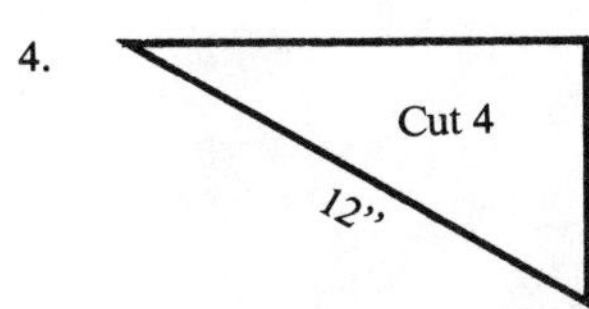

Cutting:

For each block, construct strata and press. Using your 4" template, cut triangles on base from all strata. Sew into blocks, using one #1, three #2, three #3, and a 4" triangle of plain muslin.

For the small quilt, cut from muslin:

1. Twelve short setting strips 4" wide. These are cut as a parallelogram to 60° angles using your template. Each long side measures 8".
2. Four 120° triangles (2 templates) (see page 13) whose sides measure 10-1/2".
3. Six 60° triangles (1 template) whose sides measure 8-1/4". (7-1/4" perpendicular.)
4. Four 30° triangles (1/2 template) whose long side measures 12".
5. Five long setting strips 4" wide for lattice between rows.

Directions:

Construct 18 Viola Blocks.

On a table or floor arrange your blocks until the colors please you. Then sew the short strips and blocks together in rows according to the diagram. Add the one-template triangles to the row ends at the top or bottom as shown in the diagram. (Laying your rows together on a table or the floor will help you see which fill-in triangles are needed.) Add the two-template triangles to the row ends at the sides. Construct the remaining two corner sections from one Viola block, one 60° triangle, one 120° triangle, and one 30° triangle.

Add long strips between these rows, leaving extra at the ends to be trimmed later. Sew the strips on the left of center to the left side of each row. Sew the strips on the right of center to the right side of the row. This helps eliminate errors in strip length.

When sewing rows together, Viola blocks will line up as shown in diagram. As you sew, lay each row face down on the next one so you can align seams. Pin and open rows up to be sure before sewing. When the whole top is together, press it. Trim the edges straight, leaving extra fabric beyond seam allowance. Add a strip of muslin at the bottom so the distance from the stem tips to the raw edge of the muslin is 3". This balances the white area at the top. Then add borders as desired. The quilt pictured in color on page 21 has a 1-3/4" border of print fabric and a 5" strip of unbleached muslin as the final border.

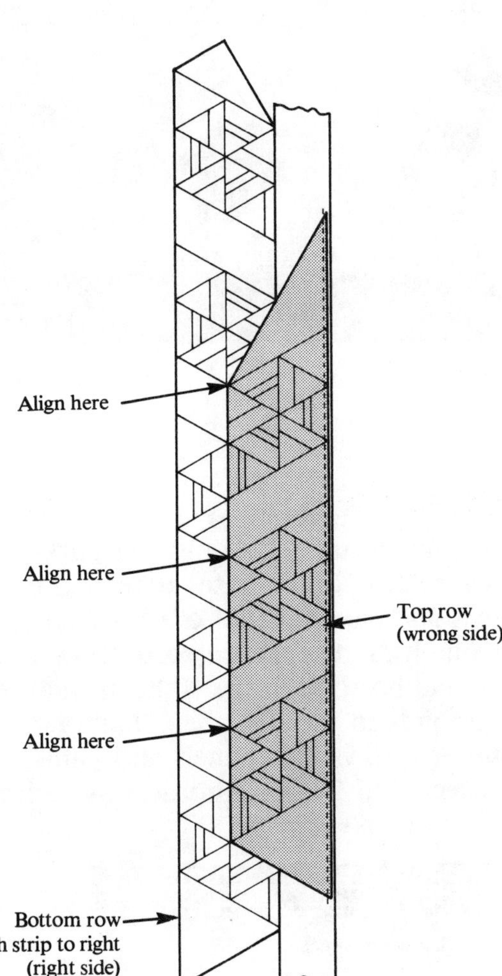

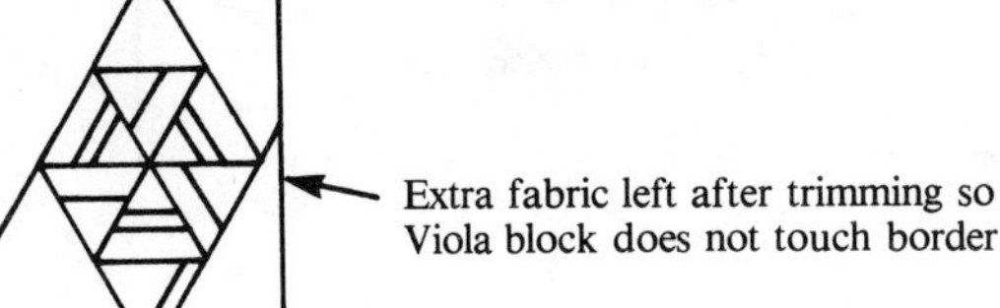

NIGHT SKY

Strip-Piecing: on base
Triangle Size: 4-1/2"
Design Size: 30" x 45" with borders

The quilt that uses the other half of this strata is "In the Clover" on page 39. Fabric requirements given make both quilts.

Strata (includes seam allowances):

2-5/8" light fabric	Strip #1
2-3/8" dark fabric	Strip #2

Fabric Requirements (for both quilts—"Night Sky" and "In the Clover"):

1-1/2 yds. light fabric
1-1/2 yds. dark fabrics of your choice

Night Sky Block

50 needed

Fill-in-Piece

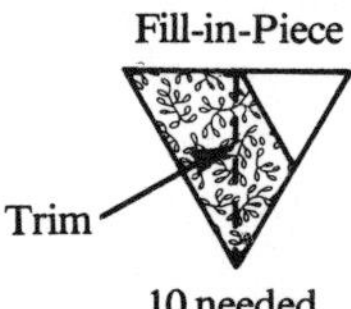

10 needed

Fill-in-Piece

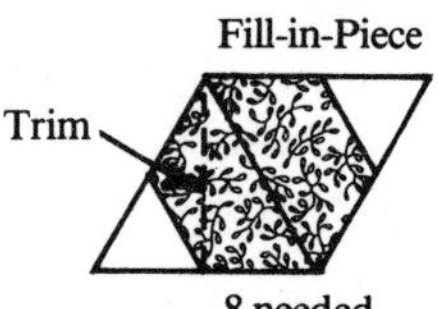

8 needed

(pictured on page 25)

Variation:

A larger quilt can be made by cutting more triangles and using a larger template. For example:

Triangle Size: 5-1/4"
Design Size: 67-1/2" x 84"
Strata (includes seam allowance):

3" light fabric	Strip #1
2-3/4" dark fabric	Strip #2

Fabric Requirements:
7 yds. light fabric
7 yds. dark fabric

Directions:

Construct strata. Press. Using your 4-1/2" template, cut triangles on base from your strata. Use only the dark-based triangles. Sew triangles into diamonds, bases together. Before you sew the rows together, add pieces at ends of row to complete the design. Take apart one triangle and use parts to make the star point border on top and bottom. Make 10 horizontal rows of diamonds with 5 diamonds in the row. Sew diamonds into rows. Add finish pieces. Sew rows into panels and panels into top. Add star point border. Add 2" plain borders as desired.

Star point border

IN THE CLOVER

Strip-piecing: on base

This is the other half of the strata used to make "Night Sky" on page 38. Fabric requirements given there make both quilts.

Triangle Size: 4-1/2"
Design Size: 45" x 45" with borders

Strata (includes seam allowance):

2-5/8" light fabric (star point)	Strip #1
2-3/8" dark fabric (base)	Strip #2

You can use any size template you wish to make these patterns. The rule is that the star point strip must be 1/4" wider in the strata than the base strip.

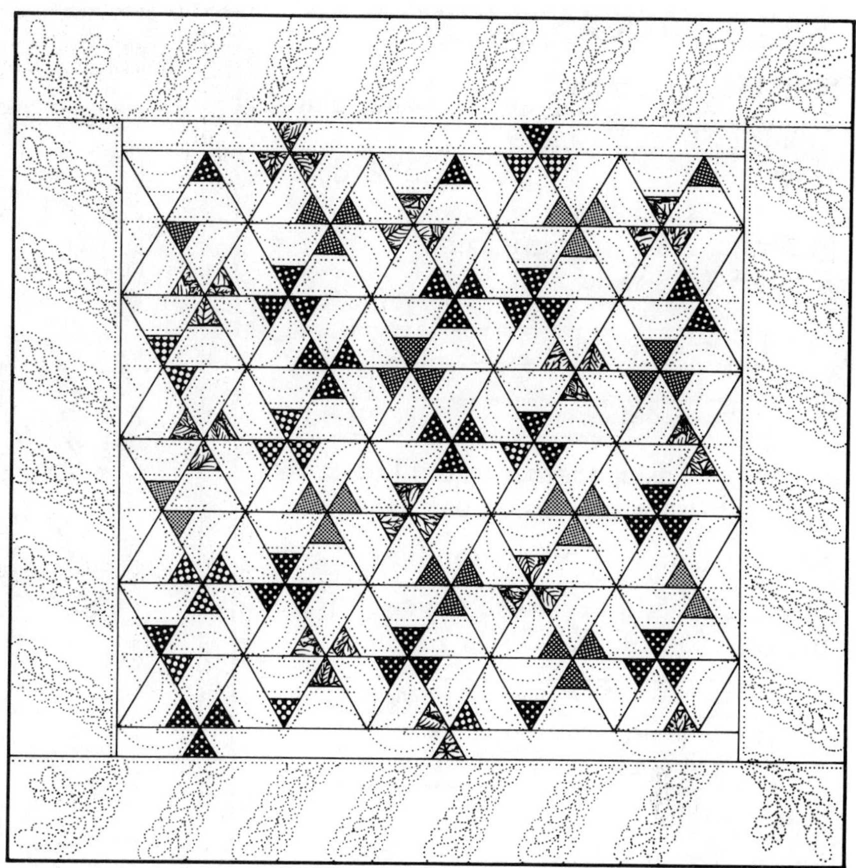

(pictured on page 25)

Directions:

Use only the light-based triangles. Arrange as pictured and sew into diagonal rows, finishing each diagonal row with a piece of fabric that can later be trimmed to the angle shown. Sew the rows together. Add a pieced border at the top and bottom to complete the sets of 3 clover leaves. Add plain borders as desired. I used 6" strips of muslin for borders.

The muslin allows the detail of a luxurious quilting design to be easily seen. The dotted lines on the diagram indicate the quilting design I used.

SAILBOATS AND ICEBERGS

Strip-piecing: on base and perpendicular
Triangle Sizes: 5" and 9"
Design Size: 48" x 57-1/2" with borders

#1 Strata: Sails—perpendicular
Strata 5-7/8" wide

3" unbleached muslin	Strip #1
7/8" mast	Strip #2
3" unbleached muslin	Strip #3

(To avoid waste, another method of constructing strata is given on page 18)

#2 Strata: Boat + Water (on base)

Strata 5" wide (You will have leftover triangles for another design.)

2-1/8" red (or boat color)	Strip #1
3/4" white (for the bow wave)	Strip #2
3-1/8" dark blue (water)	Strip #3

Fabric Requirements:
- 2" x 45" solid color for mast.
- 1/2 yd. assorted red stripe, check, or print for boats and first border
- 1 yd. dark blue for water
- 1-3/4 - 2 yds. blue for sky and third border
- 2 yds. unbleached muslin and assorted fabrics for icebergs and second border

For each block: 9" Template—cut one triangle of unbleached muslin, light blue stripes, black polka dots, etc.

5" Template—cut two triangles of sky color, one triangle for sails, and one for boat and water

Sailboats and Icebergs Block

16 needed

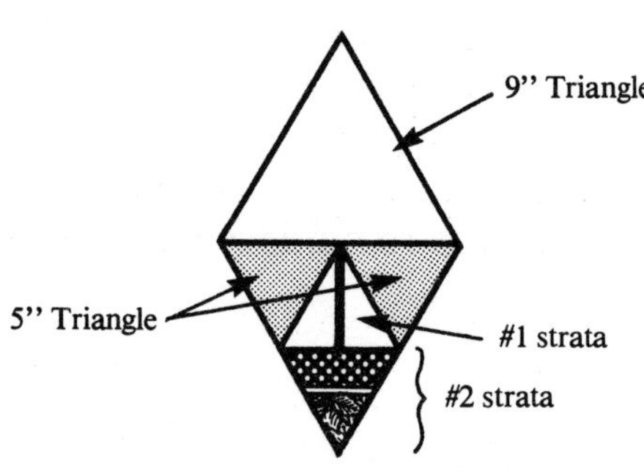

(pictured on page 22)

Directions:

Construct strata. Press. Cut perpendicular triangles from Strata #1. Cut on base triangles from Strata #2. Piece 14 blocks and 2 partial blocks. Cut half-template pieces 10-1/2" on long side: 4 sky blue + 4 muslin. Sew blocks together in rows, adding half-template pieces at the ends of rows, top and bottom. Sew rows together. Trim edges straight. Add borders. When measuring for borders, measure across the horizontal and vertical center to determine length, as all the edges are bias.

Cut borders:
- 1st border — 1-3/4" wide
- 2nd border — 4" wide
- 3rd border — 2" wide

Cut the borders to the proper length and pin, matching centers, ends, and quarters. Then sew.

SNOWSTORM

Strip-piecing: on base and perpendicular
Triangle Size: 4"
Design Size: 54-1/2" x 66-1/2" with borders
No strata given
Fabric Requirements: (Polka dots and stripes are desirable.)

The Snowflakes:
(small amounts of all)
- 4 red prints or solids
- 2 aqua prints
- 6 light blue or blue and white prints
- 1 purple/violet print
- Some of the background fabrics

The Background:
- 1-1/2 yds. of dark navy large print, swirly with some white and blue
- 1 yd. navy
- 1/2 - 1 yd. each of 2 busy medium spotty prints
- 1/2 - 1/4 yd. each of 2 dark blue pindots

(pictured on page 23)

Directions:

Utilize scraps in this design. My navy blue is actually four different dark colors, one a strong blue cotton satin. Make it like a painting. I appliqued hexagons over the centers of three of the snowflakes.

Piece the snowflakes first, but do not sew them together. Lay them out on a flat surface and fill in spaces until you can piece together a full diamond, triangle, or parallelogram. Sew these together with other large units, pieced or whole cloth shapes, which you have cut out, using larger templates and rulers. When the whole panel is pieced, add a wide dark border on the top and left side and a wide medium border on the bottom and right side. (Notice how the border is pieced.)

The quilting pattern is geometric on the snowflakes with spiral swirls and curved lines on the remainder of the quilt.

SHOOTING STARS

Sandwich-piecing: matching triangles
Triangle Size: 4"
Design Size: 71-1/2" x 101"

Borders can be added and will make the quilt larger, or you may finish with a jagged edge. Try this as a multi-colored quilt.

Fabric Requirements:

For block centers
- 2 yds. muslin
- 1 yd. other light color

For block points
- 1-1/4 yds. assorted dark colors (twelve 3-3/4" strips)

For block borders
- 4 yds. assorted medium colors

1/4 yd. of 2 fabrics, 42" wide, made into matching triangles, can give up to 32 pairs, if everything is on straight of grain with no flaws.

Shooting Stars Block

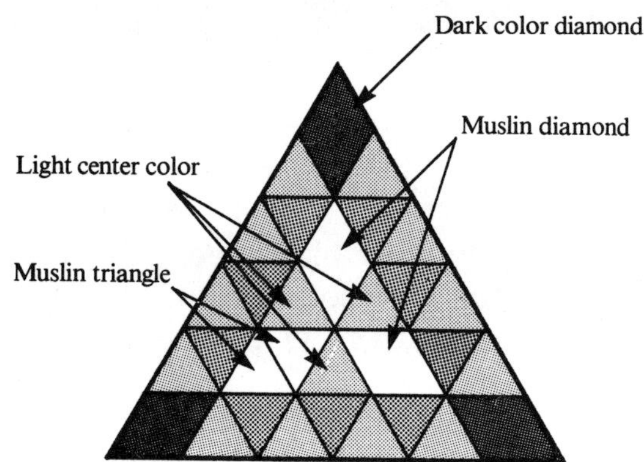

You will need 21 whole blocks and 15 partial blocks.

Piece this block in rows.
Placement for matching triangles

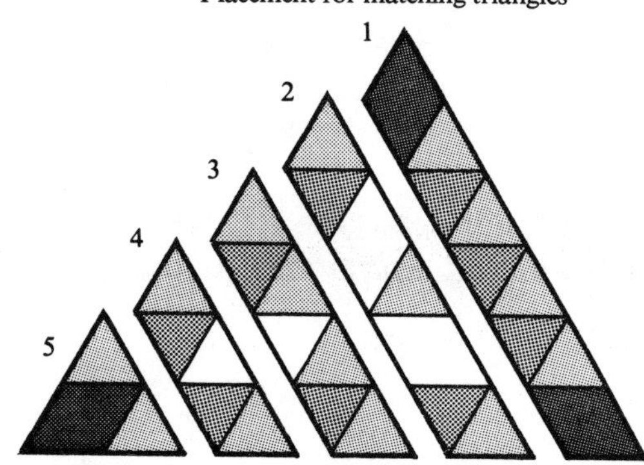

(pictured on page 26)

Directions:
Cut from muslin: 21 triangles (from 4" strips)
42 diamonds (from 3-3/4" strips - see p. 13)
Cut from other center color: 54 triangles (from 4" strips)
Sandwich-piece from center colors:
36 pairs of matching triangles (from 4" strips)
Cut from the dark colors:
63 diamonds (from 3-3/4" strips)
Sandwich-piece from border colors:
297 pairs of matching triangles (from 4" strips)

Piece your blocks from these units. As you piece, you will need to cut 63 triangles, selecting border colors to complete the color scheme of your block. Add three 4" triangles in the lighter border color to each block. Arrange the blocks in vertical rows and sew together. Construct partial blocks for the side borders and the top and bottom ends of rows and add to complete the panels. Then sew these panels together.

RAZZLE DAZZLE

Sandwich-piecing: half-triangle
Triangle Size: 6"
Design Size: 73-1/2" x 91"

Fabric Requirements:

1-1/2 yds. each of 2 colors in dark block
1-1/3 yds. each of 2 colors in light block
1-1/2 yds. each of 2 colors in medium block
Total yardage: 8-2/3 yds.
(Makes a quilt and its reverse)

Razzle Dazzle Block

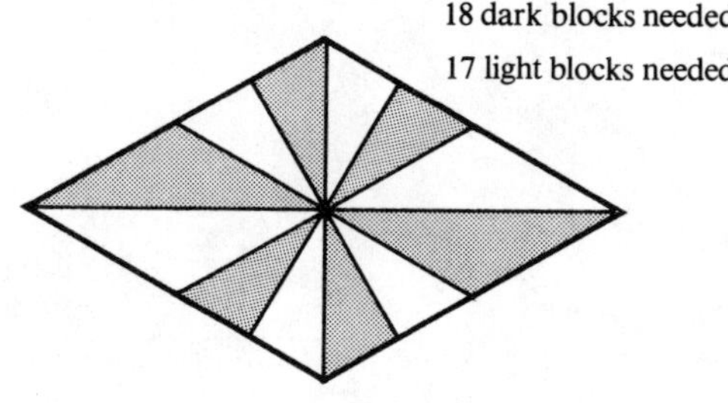

Razzle Dazzle Half Block

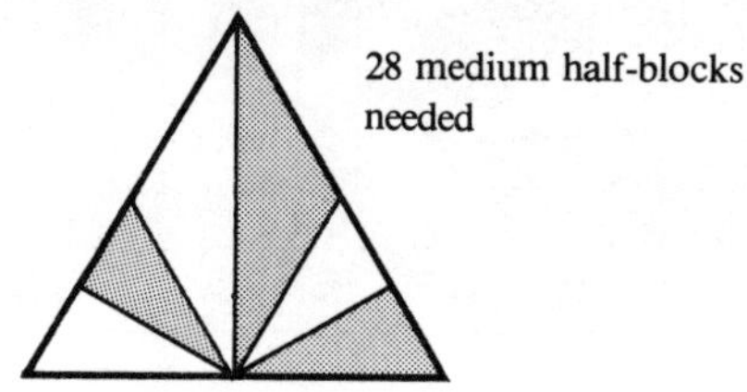

Piecing sequence

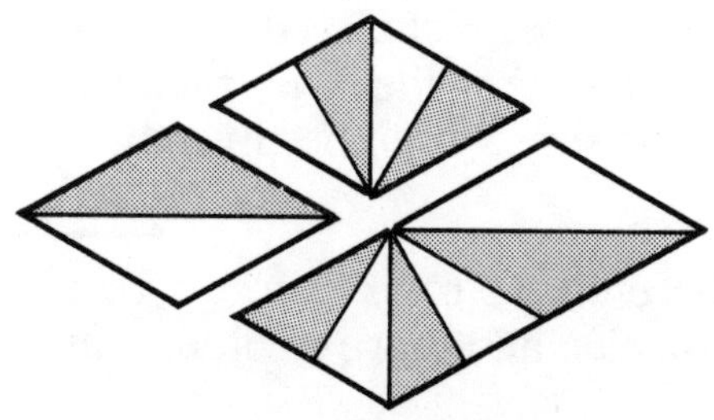

(pictured on page 25)

Directions:

Make half-diamonds and half-triangles in color combinations of light, medium, and dark value. Sew into half blocks and blocks. You will have reverse waste units to use in another project.

Sew 5 blocks and 4 half blocks alternately into each row. Make ends of rows square with quarter blocks in medium colors.

Example: One Row with 5 Blocks and 4 Half Blocks

GRANNY SQUARE

Sandwich-piecing: half-triangle
Triangle Size: 5''
Design Size: 61-3/4'' x 91-1/4'' with borders

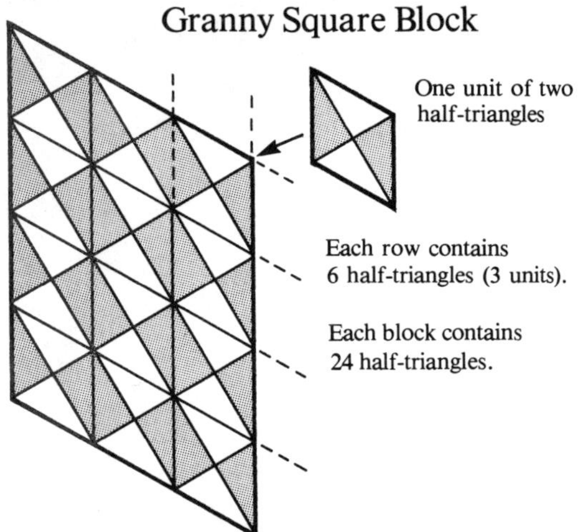

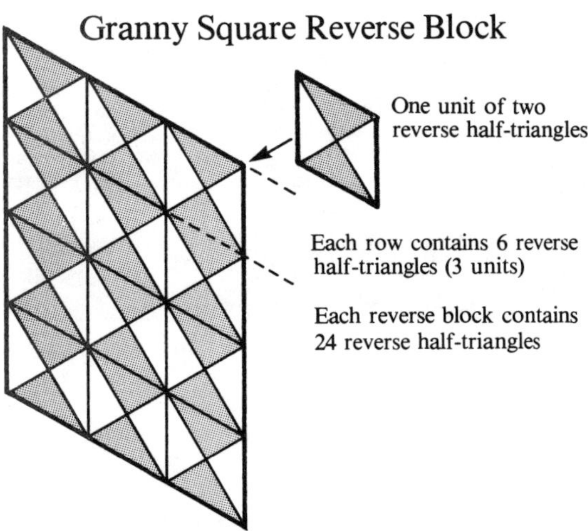

Fabric Requirements (approximately):
- 3 yds. light assorted colors
- 3 yds. dark assorted colors

There are 22 half-triangles in every 5-1/2'' x 42'' pair of fabric strips in light/dark combination for sandwich piecing. There might be 408 half-triangles in this whole quilt. Nineteen pairs of strips should supply enough half-triangles for the whole quilt.

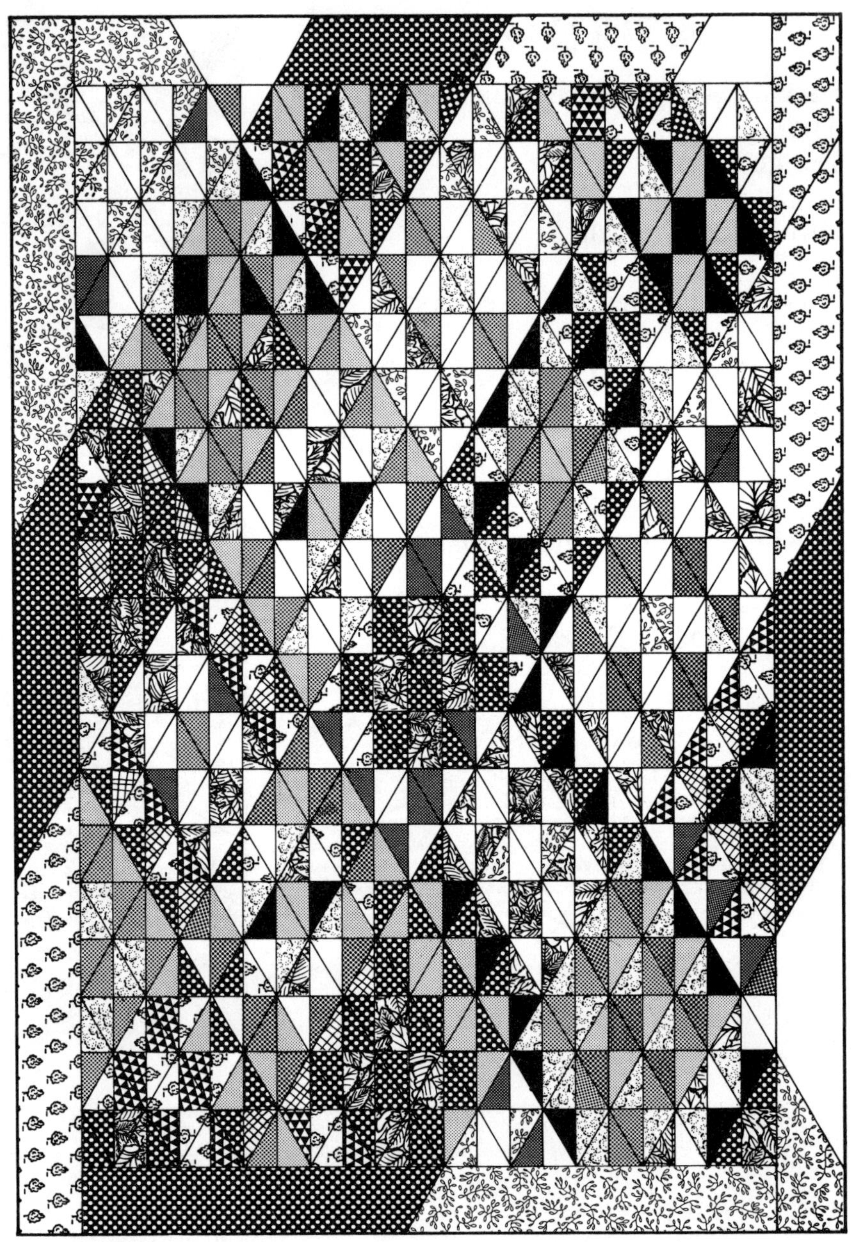

(pictured on page 27)

Directions:

Sandwich-piece half-triangles in dark/light combinations and arrange them in granny square blocks. Make partial blocks as necessary. Fill in the right and left sides with pieces of extra half-triangles taken apart and sewed together like this:

Sew these segments on the ends of rows before assembly of partial blocks. Arrange blocks and partial blocks and sew together.

For geometrically pieced border, cut fabric used in quilt in 5-1/2'' wide strips and lay along edge of quilt top. Match values carefully to produce a light or dark background and to bring out movement of colors from quilt top.

Use your triangle template to mark the angle on the border that continues the line of color from the quilt top. Top and bottom angles should be 60° and the sides 30°.

GOLD STAR

Sandwich-piecing: half-diamonds and (optional) matching triangles
Triangle size: 4"
Design size: 45-1/2" x 56-1/4"

Gold Star Block

29 complete blocks needed

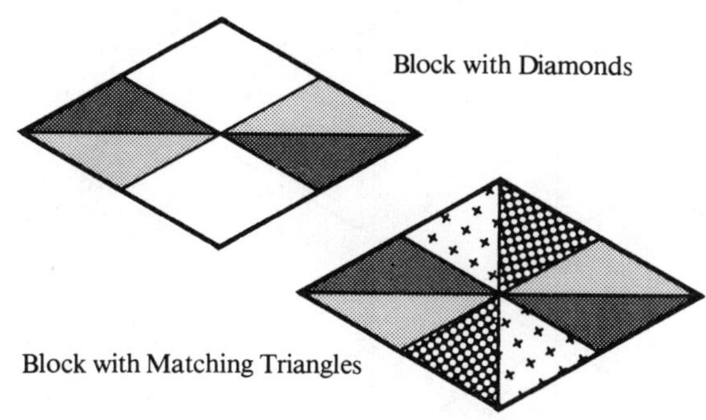

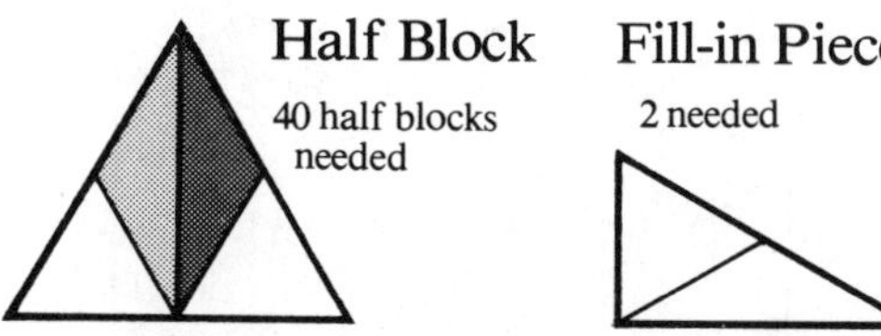

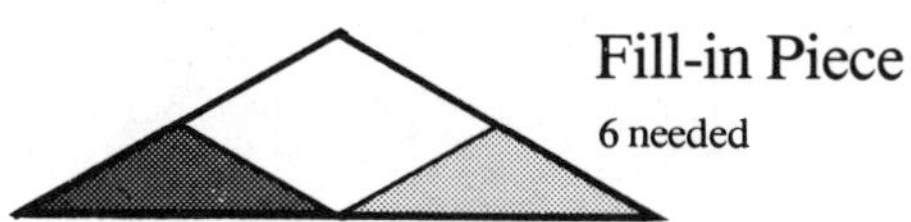

Fabric Requirements:

1 yd. bright yellow
1 yd. black prints or solids
Background colors (approximately 1 yd. total)

red	pale pink
peach	light blue
pink	muslin

(pictured on page 26)

Directions:

Sandwich-piece 98 half-diamonds according to the directions on page 29. Sandwich-piece matching triangles as desired or cut diamonds from the background color(s). Cut diamonds and triangles to complete blocks and half-blocks.

Piece the blocks and half-blocks and sew together into rows according to the diagram. Make fill-in pieces for the ends of the rows, top and bottom. Sew the rows together diagonally to complete the quilt top.

Example: One row with 4 blocks and 6 half blocks.

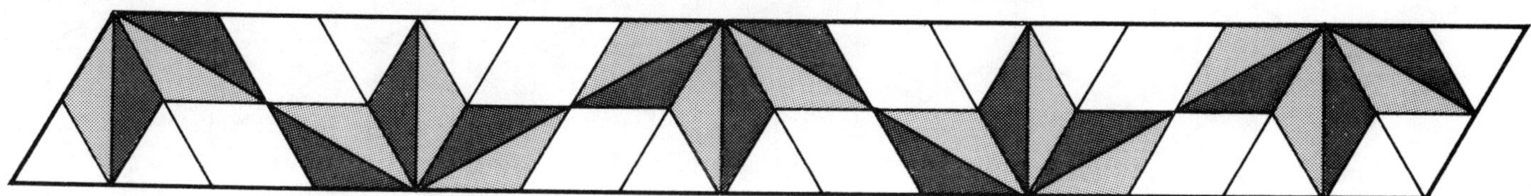

About the Author

Sara Nephew began her artistry in metalwork. After receiving a B.A. degree in Fine Art, she worked for a commercial shop, repairing and designing jewelry, and invented a new enamel-on-brass technique. Her cloisonne work has appeared in national exhibits. She has since turned her interests to quilting, in large part, because of her fascination with the myriad colors and textures of fabric. In 1984 she started her own business repairing, making, and selling quilts and wall hangings. Currently, she is designing quilts and teaching her special techniques.

Sara lives in Snohomish, Washington, with her husband, Dale, and their three children. She is active in two local quilt guilds, Quilters Anonymous and Busy Bee Quilters.

That Patchwork Place Publications

	Retail
Basics of Quilted Clothing by Nancy Martin	8.00
Bearwear by Nancy J. Martin	7.95
Branching Out-Tree Quilts by Carolann Palmer	11.95
Cathedral Window-A New View by Mary Ryder Kline	6.00
Christmas Classics by Sue Saltkill	6.95
Christmas Quilts by Marsha McCloskey	11.95
Country Christmas by Sue Saltkill	6.00
Fabriscapes™ by Gail Johnson	5.00
Feathered Star Sampler by Marsha McCloskey	3.95
Housing Projects by Nancy J. Martin	9.95
Linens and Old Lace by Nancy Martin and Sue Saltkill	9.95
Make a Medallion by Kathy Cook	12.95
More Template-Free Quiltmaking by Trudie Hughes	12.95
Pieces of the Past by Nancy J. Martin	18.95
Projects for Blocks and Borders by Marsha McCloskey	11.95
Quilter's Christmas by Nancyann Twelker	8.00
Sew Special by Susan A. Grosskopf	6.00
Small Quilts by Marsha McCloskey	6.00
Stencil Patch by Nancy Martin	6.00
Template-Free Quiltmaking by Trudie Hughes	11.95
Touch of Fragrance by Marine Bumbalough	5.95
Wall Quilts by Marsha McCloskey	8.00

(Prices subject to change)